Confronting the Evolving Global Security Landscape

Confronting the Evolving Global Security Landscape

Lessons from the Past and Present

MAX G. MANWARING

Foreword by Joseph M. Humire

Praeger Security International

An Imprint of ABC-CLIO, LLC

Santa Barbara, California • Denver, Colorado

Library of Congress Cataloging in Publication Control Number: 2019006188

ISBN: 978–1–4408–6782–8 (print)
     978–1–4408–6783–5 (ebook)

23 22 21 20 19   1 2 3 4 5

This book is also available as an eBook.

Praeger
An Imprint of ABC-CLIO, LLC

ABC-CLIO, LLC
147 Castilian Drive
Santa Barbara, California 93117
www.abc-clio.com

This book is printed on acid-free paper ∞

Manufactured in the United States of America

Those who excel in war first cultivate their own humanity and justice and maintain their Laws and institutions. By these means they make their governments invincible.
—Sun Tzu, *The Art of War*

Contents

Foreword

by Joseph M. Humire

Turn on the news any day of the week and you will see endless crime and violence by gangs, cartels, terrorists, insurgents, and other armed non-state actors in close to every corner of the world. Wars and civil conflicts are raging in Syria, Venezuela, Congo, Yemen, Myanmar, South Sudan, and more, while the United States is increasingly stretched thin in Iraq and Afghanistan. According to the UN Refugee Agency, there are more refugees today than after World War II, yet no nation is in a declared conventional war with another nation-state.

Wars and conflict continue to be a growing phenomenon, but today's wars are not like those of earlier generations. The strength of an adversary no longer lies in its military capability, and the root cause of most asymmetric threats rests in malgovernance and failed institutions within society. This lesson is a central point in the writings and teachings of Dr. Max Manwaring, who is a leading authority on irregular warfare. Whether you call modern-day conflicts asymmetric, unconventional, irregular, or as General John Galvin coined in his 1986 classic *Uncomfortable Wars: Towards a New Paradigm*—today's battlefield looks less like Normandy and more like Mogadishu. Unless we change our thinking on how to approach modern warfare, our fate is to endure the perils of never-ending small wars that ultimately drain our blood and treasure.

Herein lies the importance of this book. Among many lessons, it has one important takeaway: to achieve sustainable security we must address the root causes of a conflict.

Take, for instance, that the deadliest place on the earth is in the tapering isthmus of a subregion called the Northern Triangle of Central America, leading the world in homicides year after year. Menaced by corruption, drug trafficking, organized crime, and gang violence, the United States has provided the governments of the three countries in the Northern Triangle billions in aid over the past decade to apply a military-law enforcement approach to the problem. To date, official statistics show that crime and violence trends have not changed as the U.S. and regional policy makers only address the symptoms of insecurity and ignore the root causes of it. And perhaps the most fundamental of those throughout Central America is the relative decline of economic freedom.

The policy-making community often neglects economics as part of a national security strategy to deal with contemporary conflicts. This volume takes a reader from security to stability, onto development and responsible governance, ultimately to strengthen sovereignty to achieve peace. Dr. Manwaring carefully explains each of the interrelated, circular components of multidimensional security. Each component is accompanied by an empirical example to emphasize its relevance to postconflict success. This book is a culmination of all that I have learned over the years from Dr. Manwaring, whom I am privileged to call a friend and a mentor.

Shortly after leaving an eight-year stint in the U.S. Marines, which included combat tours in Iraq, I studied economics at George Mason University, a school renowned for its economic scholars, which includes two Nobel laureates. After college, I found myself yearning for more knowledge on what makes societies prosperous but also peaceful. In 2008, I entered the world of think tanks, working initially at a foundation where I met Dr. Manwaring and his son, Alan, when we embarked on an international journey to teach the proverbial "Manwaring Paradigm" to a new generation of national security leaders in Colombia, Guatemala, Chile, Argentina, Georgia, and the Czech Republic. Many of these leaders now hold important positions in their countries and are fighting alongside the United States against shared threats to international security.

I have now been in the industry for almost a decade, leading a national security think tank whose mission is in its name—Center for a Secure Free Society (SFS). Considered an expert on counterterrorism and transnational threats in the Western Hemisphere, I have testified before various committees in Congress and Parliaments worldwide, regularly briefed several ministers and military/intelligence leaders of regional allies, and published my own book in 2014, addressing the asymmetric threat posed by Iran and Hezbollah in Latin America. More importantly, I am one of many in a new generation of national security experts taught by Dr. Manwaring to examine conflicts from a multidimensional and societal perspective using the tenants of asymmetric war and applying them to contemporary national security challenges.

One of these challenges and perhaps the most important for the U.S. national security is the crisis in Venezuela. Holding the world's highest inflation rate, with the largest foreign debt, and an economy that has shrunk by half—Venezuela is imploding as more than 3 million of its citizens have escaped hunger and lack of medicine, catalyzing the second largest refugee outflow in the world after Syria. Unlike other humanitarian crisis, however, Venezuela's is by design brought about by a tyrannical regime that has advanced a Marxist-Leninist-inspired revolution in the region for more than two decades. Interestingly, it was Dr. Manwaring who first warned us about this coming catastrophe back in 2005.

One of the first works I read from Dr. Manwaring was a monograph titled *Venezuela's Hugo Chavez, Bolivarian Socialism, and Asymmetric Warfare*, published in October 2005 at the Strategic Studies Institute of the U.S. Army War College, where Dr. Manwaring retired as a leading scholar. In this piece, Dr. Manwaring describes Hugo Chávez as a serious threat to the U.S. national security and warned that his Bolivarian revolution is spreading throughout Latin America. Dr. Manwaring's analytical perspective, however, flew in the face of Washington's policymakers who at the time chose to ignore the Venezuelan *caudillo* because they viewed his fiery rhetoric as more bark than bite. As Dr. Manwaring described, Chávez became analogous to Lord Voldemort from the Harry Potter series, as he turned out to be "He Who Must Not Be Named" as a matter of U.S. policy for almost a half-decade.

Dr. Manwaring's warning proved prophetic, and by 2009, Chávez's Bolivarian Revolution had captured the targeted governments in Bolivia, Nicaragua, Ecuador, and several satellite countries in the Caribbean. It also linked to other like-minded revolutions and regimes in Iran, Syria, Russia, China, and North Korea. In 2012, Dr. Manwaring published a follow-up monograph called *Venezuela as an Exporter of 4th Generation Warfare Instability*, which foresaw the calamity that Venezuela has become today.

This latest book by Dr. Manwaring is more than just theory. It has real-world implications. Venezuela has now become one of the most complex *hybrid* conflicts in the evolving global security arena—mixing state and nonstate actors, using a combination of lethal and nonlethal attacks, aimed at destabilizing the entire Americas while delegitimizing the United States. Solving this national security challenge will require more than hard or soft power; it will require "smart power" and a whole-of-society approach that begins with understanding the hard learned, but often ignored, lessons from the past and present. This book emphasizes these lessons and is meant to inspire a new generation of national security thinkers, who, like me, heed the teachings of Dr. Manwaring, to ensure that no more "Venezuelas" occur in our lifetime or in that of our children.

Joseph M. Humire
Executive Director, Center for a Secure Free Society (SFS)
Washington, DC

Preface and Acknowledgments

The present-day global security situation is characterized by an unconventional spectrum of conflict that no one from the traditional Westphalian school of thought would recognize or be comfortable with. In addition to conventional attrition war conducted by easily recognized military forces of another nation-state, we see something considerably more complex and ambiguous. Regardless of any given politically correct term for war or conflict, all state and nonstate actors involved in any kind of conflict are engaged in one common political act—that is, war. The intent is to control and/or radically change a government and to institutionalize the acceptance of an aggressor's objectives and values. It is important to remember that these "new" actors and "new" types of battlefields are being ignored or, alternatively, they are considered too complicated and ambiguous to deal with. Yet, they seriously threaten the security, stability, development, and well-being of all parts of the global community.

Thus, the purpose of this book is to draw from the lessons of history to better prepare today's civilian, military, opinion leaders, and voters for the unconventional and asymmetric (i.e., hybrid) warfare challenges that are increasingly faced by the United States and the rest of the global community. Each case has much to teach. Contemporary conflict is not a "business as usual" ad hoc exercise. It is a deadly and long-term exercise in survival. And, importantly, this is a beginning point from which civilian and military leaders, policy makers, opinion makers, and responsible citizens might generate the broad strategic vision necessary to win a war—not just the battles but the war itself.

This book is the direct result of an invitation to conduct a series of seminars at the Chilean Army War College. I did not do the seminars but thanks to General Humberto Oviedo Arriagada, commander in chief of the Chilean Army, and Colonel Arturo Contreras Polgatti (Ret., Chilean Army), I was encouraged to write this book. Then, like so many authors, I am deeply grateful to the "usual suspects" whose influence, knowledge, experience, wisdom, support, and patience have helped make this book possible. Acknowledging and thanking every person who has contributed somewhere somehow to the thinking and writing process, however, is impossible. Nevertheless, I would be remiss if I did not single out Ambassador Edwin G. Corr, General John R. Galvin (Ret., U.S. Army), Colonel Robert M. Herrick (Ret., U.S. Army), and Lt. Colonel John T. Fishel (Ret., U.S. Army). These individuals have constantly encouraged me in this effort. Additionally, a few others should be acknowledged. They include Professor Douglass C. Lovelace Jr., Dr. Robert J. Bunker, and Dr. W. Andrew Terrill of the Strategic Studies Institute of the U.S. Army War College. They have helped make me appear to be more knowledgeable and articulate than I really am. In that connection, I respectfully and lovingly dedicate this book to my wife, Janet. She is my rock, my light, and my life. At the same time, given the security threats and challenges that all of our children and grandchildren face now and in the future, I would like to note that this book is for my five-year-old grandson, Will.

Lastly, all statements of fact, opinion, or analysis are mine and do not reflect the position of any private or public institution. I, alone, am responsible for any errors of fact or judgment.

Prologue

Twenty-five hundred years ago, Sun Tzu taught the broad grand-strategic vision within which weaker state and nonstate actors might operate against stronger adversaries. An explanation of that vision begins with the notion that the primary means through which the enlightened prince and wise generals subdue the enemy is foreknowledge. What is called foreknowledge is obtained from individuals who know the enemy situation. Then, once that foreknowledge is understood, "what is of supreme importance is to attack the enemy's strategy." Sun Tzu's narrative tells us that "all the generals said, 'This is beyond our comprehension.'"[1] We do not know what happened next, but I will take a literary leap of logic and assume that the enlightened prince sacked those generals and replaced them with civilian and military leaders who understood what Prussian general Carl von Clausewitz would write several hundred years later—that is, there are more effective ways to attack an enemy strategy than the conventional military-centric wars of attrition.[2] The military-centric approach to security has proven relatively ineffective in terms of achieving long-term peace and stability objectives. On the other hand, strong empirical evidence demonstrates that a people-centric whole-of-government approach to peace and security that equates to what Professor Joseph Nye calls "smart power" would be very close to what Sun Tzu wanted to hear from his generals.[3]

To help civilian and military leaders, opinion makers, scholars, and interested citizens come to grips with the realities of the contemporary global security arena, this book seeks to do four things. First, I briefly outline the evolution of the national and international security concept from

1648 and the Treaty of Westphalia to the present. Second, I examine the circular and upward relationship of the elements that define contemporary security. Third, I accompany the discussion of each element—security, stability, development, governance, sovereignty, and back again to security—with empirical examples from around the world. Last, I caution the reader that people-centric approaches to achieve security are required if the United States is to play more effectively in the international security arena now and in the future. Accordingly, the strategic purpose of this book goes beyond an attempt to address major gaps in the national and international security literature. The fundamental relevance and imperative of this book lie in the transmission of hard-learned, but too often ignored, lessons from the past and present.

CHAPTER 1

Introduction, Method, and Lessons from the Portuguese Coup of 1974

Political and military leaders and opinion makers all around the world have been struggling with "new" indirect and ambiguous political, sociopsychological, and military aspects of security since at least the dissolution of the Soviet Union. Yet, the nature of the contemporary security phenomenon is still not well understood. New actors and new types of conflict are being ignored or, alternatively, are considered too complicated and ambiguous to deal with. Consequently, that phenomenon seriously threatens the security, stability, and general well-being of all or some parts of the global community.

This introductory chapter outlines the changing nature of the national and international security concepts. The main themes that run through the international politics literature and foreign and defense policy stress the following: (1) the evolution of the security concept, (2) the development of a holistic people-centric security equation, and (3) the case study methodology. Additionally, we provide (4) an accompanying vignette that illustrates the security aspects of Portugal's transition from a failed dictatorship to a model of liberal Western democracy.

THE EVOLUTION OF THE CONCEPT OF SECURITY—
A BIT OF ESSENTIAL HISTORY

The Traditional Concept of Security

Several international relations texts teach that the bloody international anarchy of seventeenth-century Europe generated a determination on the part of the controlling elites to devise an interstate system that would prevent anything like the Hundred Years' War from happening again. The negotiations resulted in the Treaty of Westphalia in 1648. The major powers of the day pledged to honor other nation-states' complete control over the territory and people affirmed to be theirs. That was defined as state sovereignty, considered sacrosanct, and also defined as national security. Intervention by one nation-state in the domestic or foreign affairs of another country was defined as aggression.

Aggression or defense against aggression was, and is still, defined as "protective" or "preventative." The notion of protective defense has tended to focus on the military-centric protection of a nation's territory, people, and specific interests abroad. That is legal under international law. Preventative defense that addresses preemptive or "anticipatory" actions that would preclude a direct threat from a nation-state adversary is also considered to be aggression. To add more confusion to this diplomatic rhetoric, preemptive action is illegal but may be considered legitimate. Offensive and/or defensive aggression can be strongly supported by propaganda, information, moral warfare, and a combination of other types of conflict that might include, but are not limited to, psychological war, financial war, trade war, cyber war, diplomatic war, proxy war, narco-criminal war, and guerrilla (i.e., insurgency) war. There are no ways or means that cannot be combined with others. In any event, in the past or at present, defenders and aggressors tend to claim to be acting in defense of real or perceived sovereign security interests, and thus their actions are appropriate in terms of international law.

The reality of the situation was, and still is, that there is no entity in the anarchic global security arena that is strong enough to enforce what is called international law. Better we think in terms of international guidelines. Thus, from the time of the Treaty of Westphalia to the present, the security concept was defined as sovereignty. Sovereignty and security became synonymous and continued to be defined as control of a well-defined national territory and the people in it. Security was also defined as protection against or prevention of harm to the national sovereignty. Further elaboration has defined national security and sovereignty as military, economic, and/or diplomatic protection against, or prevention of, perceived aggression against a given nation-state.[1]

To add a little more confusion to the problem, the stability concept has come into the security-sovereignty lexicon and has been sometimes confused with the idea of security. More often than not, these terms have also been used synonymously and defined as protection of territory and people. In any event, the definition of security has been expanded. It now includes the task of generating responsible governance, that is, Ambassador Stephen Krasner's "responsible sovereignty."[2] Stability, on the other hand, has become the foundational element that enables national and international socioeconomic-political development and provides the bases for a liberal democracy and a sustainable peace. (Note the Peace-Security Paradigm later in the chapter.)

Further Change and Development of the Security Concept

More recently, security and conflict have become even more complex and ambiguous. In 1996, the secretary general of the United Nations, Boutros Boutros-Ghali, described the most important dialectic at work in the post–Cold War world as globalization and fragmentation. He observed that globalization was creating a world that has become increasingly interconnected and a positive force for decolonization, good government, socioeconomic development, human rights, and improving the environment. The secretary general too understood that that dialectic was acting as a negative fragmenting force, leading people everywhere to seek refuge in smaller, more homogeneous groups characterized by isolation, separatism, fanaticism, and proliferation of intrastate conflict. He also recognized that that kind of fragmentation can act as an important cause—related to poverty, social exclusion, and malgovernance—of state failure.

As a consequence, the secretary general introduced two new types of threats—in addition to conventional preventative military, economic, and/or diplomatic aggression—into the global security arena. They are the following: (1) a new set of players that includes insurgents, transnational criminal organizations, terrorists, private armies, militias, and gangs that are taking on roles that were once reserved for traditional nation-states and (2) indirect and implicit threats to stability and human well-being such as unmet political, economic, and social expectations. As noted earlier, over a relatively short period of time, the concept of state and personal security became more than simple nation-state control of territory and people. Responsible sovereignty and the principles of protective and preventive defense would also become the task of the international community to protect and/or prevent peoples from egregious harm. Importantly, this broadened concept of security ultimately depends on eradication of the causes, as well as the perpetrators, of instability.[3]

In response to the secretary general's vision of contemporary reality, the United Nations outlined an agenda for 2030. It provided 169 ambitious, but "sustainable," development goals for nation-state and international community action over the next several years. Seventeen specific goals were designated as priority efforts. All in all, Agenda 2030 would set the conditions for elaboration of the principles of protection and prevention of peoples from harm perpetrated by governments, nonstate actors, and/or root cause stressors. In addition, the Organization of American States' (OAS) Declaration on Security of 2003 supplemented the Agenda 2030 with a list of threats to international security that included everything, and more than, the United Nations required. The new list of external and internal threats to global security and stability includes the global drug problem, trafficking in persons, attacks on cybersecurity, natural and human-made disasters, health risks, environmental degradation, and virtually all the ever-present root causes of instability. All of these dictate a fundamental change from a military-centric to a multidimensional people-centric responsible sovereignty approach to the security-sovereignty concept.[4]

A New Sociology of Security

Sovereignty (i.e., security) in the past was the unquestioned control of territory and the people in it. Security is now conditional. It is the national and international responsibility to generate the stability and well-being that enables political-economic-social development and also enables liberal democracy and a sustainable peace. This is not simply a moral-human concern. Boutros Boutros-Ghali would remind us that the new international legal principles of protection and prevention of harm, and the accompanying redefinition of security and sovereignty, are intended to preclude a coerced transition of extant values of a given society to the unwelcome values of a given winner. At the same time, a forced transition of values poses an existential threat to national and international security. Importantly, the forced transition of values is the traditional definition of war.[5] As a consequence, new players and new practices in the global security arena dictate a new sociology of security and a redefinition of the major characteristics of contemporary conflict. A few of these defining characteristics would include the following:

- The center of gravity (i.e., the hub of all power and movement on which everything depends) is no longer an easily identified military force. It is now leadership and public opinion—and the fight takes place among the people, not on a conventional virtually uninhabited battlefield.
- The broadened concept of security (i.e., responsible sovereignty) ultimately depends on eradication of causes, as well as perpetrators, of instability.
- The primary objective of contemporary security is no longer the control of sovereign territory and the people in it. The strategic objective is to capture the imagination of the people and the will of their leaders—thereby winning a public opinion trial of relative moral strength.
- The principal tools of contemporary conflict are now the proactive and coercive use of words, images, symbols, perceptions, ideas, and dreams.
- War is now total in terms of scope, method, objective, and time.
- There are the following three rules: (1) only the foolish fight fair; (2) there are no rules; and (3) the only viable morality within the anarchy of the world disorder is national self-interest.[6]

General Rupert Smith (Ret., UK) is straightforward: "War no longer exists. Confrontation, conflict and combat undoubtedly exist all around the world. ... Nonetheless, war as cognitively known to most non-combatants, war as a battle in a field between men and machinery, war as a massive deciding event in a dispute in international affairs: such war no longer exists."[7] Even so, Qiao and Wang (i.e., Qiao Liang and Wang Xiangsui) remind us that a war in which bloodshed and brutality may be reduced (e.g., cyber war) is still a war. "It may alter the cruel process of war, but there is no way to change the essence of war, which is one of compulsion, and therefore it cannot alter its cruel outcome either."[8]

DEVELOPMENT OF A HOLISTIC PEOPLE-CENTRIC SECURITY EQUATION

Boutros Boutros-Ghali's Dialectic at Work

As a result of the gravity of contemporary global security threat, we now see the international legal and security communities seriously considering Ambassador Krasner's orienting principle of responsible sovereignty. This principle is a synthesis of traditional state versus state threats, as well as nonstate threats to the global community. It also becomes the theoretical basis that leads to a new synthesis of *realpolitik* and practical idealism. In turn, it is also the theoretical basis for a new thesis that enables a durable peace rather than the coerced transition from the extant values of a given polity to the unwelcome values of a given winner.[9]

Responsible sovereignty begins with the definition of politics as "the authoritative allocation of values for a society."[10] The state and its governance (i.e., authoritative allocation of values) becomes the primary (i.e., dependent) variable and the defining element in operationalizing the concept of contemporary security. Thus, the type of governance—legitimate or not, positive or negative—is the critical variable that determines stability or instability, development or stagnation, prosperity or poverty, and peace or conflict. This, then, becomes a new synthesis. The new antithesis would be something that attempts to destroy responsible sovereignty. Even so, responsible sovereignty can overcome that antithesis by removing the political-economic-social-environmental motives that create the antithesis in the first place. The consequent operationalization of the principle of responsible sovereignty (i.e., legitimate governance) takes us toward a holistic (i.e., multidimensional) people-centric legitimate governance security paradigm. The resultant challenge and task are nothing new and not even close to radical. They are only the logical extensions of basic security and strategy and national and international asset management.[11]

The Resultant Peace-Security Paradigm

At this point, it might be a good idea to remember that no coach in the National Football League or the National Basketball Association or the coach of an Olympic team would ever go into a season without a "philosophy" for his or her team. Neither would that coach go into any given game without a carefully thought-out and well-practiced "game plan" based on his or her philosophy. The fulfillment of a holistic, population-centric, legitimate governance and stability-security equation for national and global security consists of three principal elements. They are derived from the independent variables that define security (i.e., S). These three primary elements are as follows: (1) the coercive capacity to provide a culturally acceptable level of personal and collective stability (i.e., M), (2) the ability to generate socioeconomic development (i.e., E), and (3) the political competence and rectitude to develop a type of governance to which a people can relate and support (i.e., PC). It is heuristically valuable to portray the relationship among these elements in a mathematical formula: $S = (M + E) \times (PC)$.

The political competence component of the equation is so critical that it merits a multiplier in our proposed paradigm. The use of the multiplier means that the sum of the whole can be substantially altered by the elements that constitute national political competence. The ultimate value of the economic and coercive elements of the equation can be reduced to nothing or nearly nothing if the political competence component is absent or weak. For example, $100 \times 0 = 0$. This peace-security equation was not conceived a priori. It was developed empirically from our SWORD model (a.k.a., the Manwaring Paradigm) and warrants high confidence that the findings are universal and explain much of the reality of the contemporary security environment. For example, this model predicted an impressive 88 percent of the win/loss results of 69 cases examined and is statistically significant at the 0.001 level. That is, the chances of being wrong are only 1 in 1,000.[12]

The strategic level application of this paradigm would result in a multidimensional, population-centric understanding of the closely interrelated wars within the general war. These wars include the following: (1) a more or less conventional law-enforcement "war" against an adversary and a strong effort to guarantee the legitimate use of that force; (2) a "war" to unify a multidimensional effort within the defending or attacking actor's organizational structure that deals with conflict; (3) an "information war" to convince the populace of the moral rectitude of a given campaign; (4) a "war" to isolate an attacker from his or her internal and external support; (5) an "intelligence war" to locate and neutralize the men and women who lead, plan, and execute a given conflict; and (6) a "war" for legitimacy and the moral right of an incumbent regime to exist.

The application of the paradigm at the operational level results in a more precise definition of legitimate governance. The five variables that define and explain the legitimizing and strengthening of the state are the following: (1) free, fair, and frequent selection of leaders; (2) the level of participation in or acceptance of the political process; (3) the level of perceived governmental corruption; (4) the level of perceived individual and collective well-being; and (5) the level of regime acceptance by the major social institutions. These key indicators of moral legitimacy are not exhaustive, but they statistically explain a high percentage of the legitimacy phenomenon and provide the basic architecture for the actions necessary to assist governments in their struggle to survive, develop, and prosper. As such, these indicators constitute a strong, coherent conceptual framework from which policy, strategy, and operational efforts might flow. The degree to which a political actor effectively manages a balanced mix of these five variables enables stability, development, political competence, security, acceptance, and sustainable peace, or the reverse.

Thus, legitimate governance is defined as governance that derives its just powers from the governed. There is always the possibility that an enemy could militarily overwhelm a targeted adversary, but the assumption is that this kind of governance (i.e., legitimate political competence) can and will manage, coordinate, and sustain national political-economic-social development. That, in turn, enables the individual and collective well-being that defines stability. That stability is the foundational cornerstone on which security and a sustainable peace are built.[13]

The strategic purpose of this book, however, goes beyond an attempt to address major problems in the international politics and hegemonic/hybrid conflict literature and general security policy and strategy. The fundamental relevance and imperative of this book lie in the transmission of hard-learned, but too often ignored, lessons of the past and present. Each case has something important to teach.

The Linear-Analytic Case Study Approach to This Book

The case study method is ideal for the purposes of this book. First, there is a need for continuity. The case study method provides the means to make the various chapters of the book "hang together." Individuals who utilize this method frequently find that the study of only a few sharply contrasting instances can produce a wealth of new insights. Additionally, this research approach leads to an enhanced understanding of the architecture of successful and unsuccessful strategies—or best/worst practices—in dealing with complex contemporary hybrid conflicts. With this information, the strategic analytical commonalities and recommendations can be determined that are relevant to each case examined, as well as the larger general security phenomenon.

This takes us to the theoretical linear-analytic approach to this book. Robert K. Yin defines this approach as the traditional or standard approach to case studies. That is, the major components include the Issue and Context, the Findings and Outcome, and Conclusions and Implications. The issue and context outline the political-historical situation and answer the "What?" question; the findings and outcome answer the "Who, Why, and So What?" questions; and conclusions and implications address Key Points and Lessons Learned. These elements are closely related and overlapping in that they are mutually influencing and constitute the "cause and effect" dynamics of a given situation. Without a fundamental understanding of the answers to these questions, various types of state-supported, state-associated, and/or independent nonstate belligerence are not likely to be clearly perceived, and response to such activity may turn it into something that it is not. The "cause and effects" related to the components of the linear-analytic approach, as noted here and in the following chapters, demonstrate that associated best/worst practices are not abstract—they are real.[14]

CAUTIONARY NOTES

The days of delineating an international security and stability end-state as simple short-term self-protection, limited adherence to human rights, the election of civilian political leaders, or material compassion for a humanitarian problem are numbered. The main element of U.S. foreign policy, military management, and public diplomacy must sooner or later go beyond the old ad hoc military-centric principle of protection and prevention to the new selective people-centric principle of responsible sovereignty.

In no way does this mean that the United States must be engaged all over the world all the time. It does mean, however, that policy makers and decision makers must add another set of questions to the conventional "Who, What, Why, and So What?" questions. That new set of questions would be "What might happen *if* the United States should or should not undertake any given type of remedial international action?" The great military genius Carl von Clausewitz argued that this is first of all the strategic questions and the most comprehensive. With that "foreknowledge," the political leader and commander can establish the kind of action on which they are embarking—neither mistaking it for nor trying to turn it into something that it is not.[15] Then, they can ask, "What is the geostrategic end-state?" and "*How* can one achieve that most important objective?" This effort may not be quick, easy, or cheap to operationalize, but it has proven to be far less demanding and costly in terms of blood and treasure than continuing a military-centric "business as usual" ad hoc crisis management approach to contemporary security. Again, these geopolitical tasks do not require the

United States to be involved everywhere and at all times. On the contrary, these tasks require decision makers to be very careful and selective in choosing *if* and *how* to become involved in any given conflict situation.

The general rule would be that policy makers and decision makers must carefully calculate gains and losses, and when the case warrants, they should intervene earlier rather than later. If done earlier, the initial and intense use of low-cost diplomatic and civilian instruments of statecraft and military support units can be utilized to ensure legitimacy and stability. If done later, the initial and intense use of high-cost military combat units will generally be applied to a losing situation. Ultimately, however, the only test for involvement—whatever its form and level—is national self-interest. That, again, is the only morality within the anarchy of world disorder.[16]

One last note. There is considerable redundancy in the following chapters. Virtually, the first few pages will be repeated quite often. Security and its components are very closely related, overlapping, and continually moving in a circular pattern. Everything is related and moving around and around and around again. In addition to moving in a horizontal pattern, the peace-security paradigm can move vertically up or down, depending on its constructive or destructive utilization. Better minds than this one have been struggling with these security problems for more than a couple of hundred years. Fortunately, at this point in time and with the advantages of computer science, we can submit empirical case study data to social science testing methods and—as one example—come up with answers that only have one chance in a thousand of being wrong. Even so, if one is not comfortable with the social science methodology, the logic of the case study process argues that if too many accidents demonstrate the same phenomenon, can you still view them as accidents? No. At this point, one must admit that there are empirical rules here.

Accordingly, the strategic purpose of this book goes beyond an attempt to address major gaps in the international politics and asymmetric/hybrid conflict literature and, in general, security policy and strategy. The fundamental relevance and imperative of this book lie in the transmission of hard-learned, but too often ignored, lessons of the past and present. Each case has something important to teach.

VIGNETTE: THE PORTUGUESE COUP OF 1974: A MODEL FOR LEGITIMATE POSTCONFLICT TRANSITION

Introduction

The story of the 1974 coup that took down Antonio de Oliveira Salazar's 44-year civilian dictatorship in Portugal begins with disaffected military officers who were fighting the colonial insurgency wars in Angola, Mozambique, and Guinea-Bissau in the 1960s and early 1970s.

To be sure, the role of the military in Portuguese Africa is an interesting prologue to the narrative of Salazar's downfall but that was only of peripheral relevance. The real story was within the entire officer corps. The officer corps was the key player in the coup that deposed Salazar; it was the officer corps that prevented a leftist countercoup in 1976, and the officer corps was in the long-term transformation of Portugal from a mercantilist civilian dictatorship to a capitalist economy and a liberal Western democracy.[17]

The Political-Historical Context

After World War I, Portugal suffered the worst inflation in its modern history. That economic calamity was matched by 16 years of political turmoil brought on by the instability generated by the rise and fall of 45 different governments. In that same period, only one president of the Republic served out his full term of office. With no apparent end to the chaos in sight, the Portuguese armed forces intervened and formed a "military government" in 1926. That new government appointed a professor of economics, Antonio Salazar, as minister of finance. Subsequently, Salazar took over the ministries of interior and colonies and became the prime minister in 1932 and in 1936 assumed the portfolios of foreign affairs and war. This placed Portugal definitively under Salazar's control.[18]

Salazar was an old-school conservative mercantilist, a corporatist, a populist, and a strong Roman Catholic clericalist. He was obsessed with balancing a very small budget and did not spend money on infrastructure or much of anything constructive. He believed that piety and hard work were good for the soul. Moreover, he also believed that "excess income" and material things corrupt individuals and society. Any one of these regime characteristics would have been enough to cause ample socioeconomic and political problems—and did. In any event, Portugal was locked into poverty and lack of development. At the same time, the country was largely dependent on the export from the colonies and reexport—from Portugal—of cheap primary commodities from the colonies. Most of the population worked on small family farms in the north of the country, on large privately owned landholdings (*latifundios*) in the south, or as "guest workers" in Europe. Per capita annual income in 1960 was only $160. The standard of living in Salazar's Portugal was, therefore, more characteristic of Africa than Europe. Over the years since that time, these and other socioeconomic problems fermented to the point where the regime had to rely more and more on the "secret police" to protect it from its detractors. Then, to add another set of problems to those already mentioned, the loyalty of the officer corps began to erode.[19]

In the early 1960s through the mid-1970s, the underpaid, poorly equipped, and overextended armed forces began 13 years of thankless counterinsurgency wars against well-trained, well-equipped, and highly motivated opposition. However, it was not because of anything close to military defeat or sympathy with the insurgents' leftist political orientation that caused Salazar to lose the loyalty of the officer corps. Rather, the break between the regime and the military was the insulting implication of the government's so-called Rebelo decrees. These decrees were interpreted to mean that the regular officers had failed in their counterinsurgency duty and would be replaced by "second team" *miliciano* (militia) officers. These decrees were further interpreted as the government putting the blame on the military for political defeat in these wars. The immediate response to these decrees was the formation of a secret society of left-of-center regular officers. That was the *Movimento das Forcas Armadas* (MFA). The formation of the MFA, however, was only the immediate response. A strong majority of regular officers were developing their own agenda.

Thus, with too much imposed austerity and stability for too long and with Salazar unwilling or unable to deal with the political-psychological aspects of contemporary conflict, one should not have been too surprised when, on April 25, 1974, officers and men of the Portuguese armed forces stationed in Portugal ousted the incumbent government. Under the leadership of General Antonio de Spinola, the implementation of the coup took less than a day, only four people were killed, and "the transfer of power resembled more the abdication of a senile monarch than a military overthrow."[20]

Findings: The Main Players and Their Motives

Portugal's internal conflict situation between 1974 and 1976 was shaped by a complex mix of protagonists, each with a specific program. The main players included the MFA, the regular officer corps of the armed forces, the Leninist-oriented Communist Party of Portugal (the PCP), and the Portuguese people. The revolutionary motive of each of these protagonists was straightforward—that is, to make fundamental changes in the government, the economy, and the society. Everybody agreed that these motives required taking down the Salazar regime and replacing it with something else. There was, however, no agreement among the various players as to what "something else" might be.[21]

The MFA called for "democratic centralization" (i.e., dictatorship of the proletariat) to be achieved through an alliance of the MFA and PCP leadership. The regular officers of the armed forces wanted a liberal democratic transformation of the state and the modernization of the armed forces. The PCP was in accord with the MFA and openly called for cancellation of the long-promised elections that would create a new parliament. Additionally, the PCP openly called for government ownership of the major means of production and distribution and a class-less society. The people of all classes were becoming more and more uncomfortable with the self-proclaimed dictatorial "vanguard of the pro-letariat" MFA-PCP alliance. The Portuguese people seemed to want a freely and fairly elected Western-style parliament to run the country. "Public opinion" was expressed through the still-existing centrist political parties, the promised elections, and the armed forces.

The people demanded their long-awaited elections. The regular armed forces guaranteed those elections. Most of the MFA officers withdrew from the alliance with the PCP. The PCP leadership backed down tempo-rarily but decided to do their best to disturb and stop the elections. With the support of the armed forces, elections for a new parliament were held in April 1975. Astonishingly, 90 percent of the eligible electorate voted. The centrist democratic socialists got 37.9 percent, the moderate Popular Democratic Party came in second with 26.4 percent, and the PCP received 12.5 percent of the popular vote. The majority centrist-moderate coalition took control of the Portuguese government and began the democratic transformation of the country. That is not the end of the story, however. Despite the loss of MFA support, the PCP precipitated an ill-advised attempt to violently overthrow the freely elected parliamentary government. It was at this point that the regular armed forces exercised their long-held *Poder Moderador* (moderating power)—that is, once again, the physical and psychological power that enabled and controlled the political-economic-social transition of the Portuguese state. As a conse-quence, the hard-line Leninists never succeeded in forming a viable coali-tion of radical military officers and other left-of-center political actors that could have taken control of the country.[22]

Outcome 1: The Exercise of the *Poder Moderador*

The main players of the Portuguese Revolution of 1974 and onward were not equal. The military was "more equal" than the other protago-nists for three reasons. First, the *Poder Moderador* was derived from the long and strong *Luso*-Brazilian tradition of the armed forces' position as the king's essential constituency in the political process. Thus, as guardi-ans of the 1926 Revolution (king or no king), the armed forces could and did exercise their putative and real power. Second, the officers and men of the Portuguese armed forces understood Clausewitz's "forgotten dimensions" of asymmetric (hybrid) conflict and the powerful role of public opinion in it. Third, the military was, and is, very competent in planning, organizing, and implementing nonkinetic as well as kinetic operations. Thus, the power of the armed forces was not confined to the exercise of conventional military operations. The power of the armed forces included prudent nonkinetic tactical, operational, and geostrategic actions. That, in addition to careful planning and cogent public diplomacy, gave the armed forces a considerable advantage over its political rivals. Consequently, the Portuguese military was able to take and retain the strategic and operational initiative throughout the entire period of the transition of the country from dictatorship to democracy.[23]

General Spinola and the leadership that exercised the *Poder Moderador* during that period understood that neither proclamations nor elections created a responsible democracy. They knew that that transition effort would be a long-term process; new democratic and capitalistic institutional structures would be fragile at best; and nothing of all this would be quick, easy, or cheap. They also knew that to achieve the geostrategic objective of transforming the state, the fulfillment of a holistic, multidimensional, people-centric security initiative was absolutely imperative. Likewise, they knew from their experience in planning, operationalizing, and implementing various types of conventional and nonconventional operations that such a security imperative could be achieved. The Portuguese revolutionary leadership understood what Clausewitz's translator, Michael Howard, wrote in his discussion of *The Forgotten* (political-psychological) *Dimensions of Strategy*.[24] That would require two principal efforts. First, it would require a strong clear-eyed effort to provide the polity with an understanding of the circular relationship between security, stability, development, responsible governance, and sovereignty. That understanding would provide the foundational cognitive basis for guiding decision makers, policy makers, planners, administrators, and ordinary people toward the geopolitical objective. Second, with that understanding, planners and policy makers could define the steps necessary to achieve the geopolitical objective. That is, the end-state plan (*linha de acciaio*).[25]

Outcome 2: The *Linha de Acciaio* and the Transformation of the Portuguese State

End-state planning starts from Clausewitz's argument that conflict is a continuation of politics by other means. That concept, however, should be accompanied by two qualifying arguments. First, military violence is required only when the conditions or changes sought cannot be achieved through political-diplomatic, social-economic, and/or informational-psychological ways and means. Second, end-state planning advocates synchronization of all national or international civilian and military instruments of power to gain the most synergism from the interaction of the variables selected for action.[26] Thus, end-state planning allowed Portuguese decision makers, policy makers, and planners to think logically, in synchronized phases, about the conditions that they sought to create. The strategic-level key was to understand precisely what had to be achieved; how it could realistically be achieved; and exactly what human, physical, and nonmaterial resources would be required for the effort.[27]

Perhaps the most brilliant element in developing an appropriate and viable *linha de acciaio* was to look beyond the immediate geopolitical objective. Rather than being content with achieving the political-economic-social transformation of the Portuguese state, Spinola looked toward the kind of internal peace desired. For example, General Spinola wanted "*un Portugal renovado, democratico, livre e progressivo*" (a Portugal modernized, democratic, free, and progressive). In order to achieve that ultimate objective, he knew that social cohesion had to be rebuilt. As a consequence, Spinola's holistic people-centric paradigm was organized into four overlapping phases. They were the following: (1) stabilization, (2) regeneration of the economy and addressing the root causes of instability and state failure, (3) creation of laws and institutions for a market economy, and (4) cultivation of a civil society.[28]

The first phase of the *linha de acciaio* was stabilization. It was considered to be the most critical societal requirement of the moment, and it required taking immediate action to enforce civil law and order, feed people, restart basic public services, generate local employment, and integrate refugees and soldiers returning to Portugal from the former colonies. These were the actions that provided "security" to every member of the Portuguese society. That was the primary basis on which stabilization, popular allegiance to the state, and societal cohesion were built. At the same time, these were the essential elements that had to be in place to regenerate the economy. This takes us back to where we started. This takes us to the circular process that defines progress toward viable national security. This is the long-term process through which Portugal moved from a mercantilist dictatorship to a market economy and responsible governance. And, without responsible governance, there would have been no stability, sustainable development, or peace. Also remember that without stability, there would have been no development, responsible governance, or peace.[29]

Conclusions

The Portuguese experience with the 1974 coup that deposed the Salazar dictatorship demonstrates that principled armed forces can conduct an unconventional and legitimate insurgency—that is, a nation's armed forces can conduct a preemptive or "preventative" insurgency to protect or free a people from malgovernance of any kind. That experience is a model of relatively peaceful and prudent change. It is also an example of the use of indirect and soft intellectual "smart" power as opposed to direct and brutal physical power. The metaphor that explains this, and the slow but sure process through which the armed forces achieved a market economy and a liberal democracy, can be seen in the Portuguese bullfight.

Unlike the better known Spanish bullfight in which the *matador* (bull killer) stays on his feet and kills the bull with his sword, the Portuguese bullfighter has a completely different task. The Portuguese bull is constantly outmaneuvered and brought to a state of natural exhaustion by the skillful horsemanship of the bullfighter. With the possible exception of the youngest lieutenants, the entire officer corps had served multiple tours of duty in Africa. Virtually, every officer had come to understand that their revolutionary undertaking was much like the national bullfight. Success or failure in the revolution would lie in the demonstration of skillful political-psychological-military actions that would physically exhaust the enemy and bring the conflict to a point at which the enemy could not move. In short, a responsible sovereignty legitimacy approach, appropriate use of soft and hard power, and an organizational structure to direct and ensure that the achievement of a desired end-state are not Clausewitzan relics from nearly 200 years ago. These elements define security and are the basics of foreign policy and military asset management. In our metaphorical terms, these kinds of unconventional efforts—in their many combinations and forms—constitute the "skillful horsemanship" of the Portuguese bullfighter.

KEY POINTS AND LESSONS

Key Points

- The nature of the contemporary security phenomenon is not well understood. New actors and new types of conflict are being ignored, or, alternatively, they are considered too complicated and ambiguous to deal with.

- This is the result of a fundamental change from a military-centric to a multidimensional people-centric approach to the security-sovereignty concept. New players and new practices in the global security arena dictate a new sociology of security and a redefinition of the major characteristics of contemporary security/conflict.

- The center of gravity (i.e., the hub of all powers and movements on which everything depends) is no longer an easily identified nation-state military or proxy insurgent force. It is now leadership and public opinion. The fight takes place among the people, not on a conventional virtually uninhabited battlefield. The principal tools of contemporary conflict are now the proactive use of words, images, symbols, perceptions, ideas, dreams, and time. The only thing that has remained constant over the period since 1648 is that war (i.e., conflict) is the coerced imposition of the (usually unwelcome) values of the winner.

- The nation-state and its governance becomes the primary (i.e., dependent) variable and defining element in operationalizing the concept of contemporary security. The type of governance—legitimate or not, positive or negative—is now the crucial variable that determines stability or instability, development or stagnation, prosperity or poverty, and peace or conflict. This, then, takes us toward a holistic (i.e., multidimensional) people-centric legitimate governance security paradigm.

- The slow but sure process through which the armed forces achieved a market economy and a liberal democracy can be seen metaphorically in the Portuguese bullfight. Unlike the better known Spanish bullfight in which the *matador* (bull killer) stays on his feet and kills the bull with his sword, the Portuguese bullfighter has a completely different task. The Portuguese bull is constantly outmaneuvered and brought to a state of natural exhaustion by the skillful horsemanship of the bullfighter. The success of the armed forces in the 1974 coup and the 1976 counter-coup was the result of skillful political-psychological-military actions that would physically and mentally exhaust the enemy and bring the conflict to a point at which the enemy could not move.

- A legitimacy (i.e., responsible sovereignty) approach, appropriate use of soft and hard power, and an organizational structure to direct and ensure the achievement of a desired end-state are not aberrations from 40 or 50 years ago. This paradigm defines security and is the basis of foreign policy and military asset management. In our metaphorical terms, this kind of unconventional effort—in its many combinations and forms—constitutes the "skillful horsemanship" of a Portuguese bullfighter.

- Lastly, this case provides an example of armed forces institutions acting as a force for democracy and a forerunner of new solutions to much of the international turbulence emerging out of the growing popular disillusionment with the generally poor performance of many contemporary "elected" governments.

Lessons

The Portuguese experience with the 1974 coup that deposed the Salazar dictatorship demonstrates that principled armed forces can conduct an unconventional and legitimate insurgency—that is, a nation's armed forces can conduct a "protective" or "preventative" insurgency to protect or free a people from malgovernance of any kind. That experience is a model of relatively peaceful and prudent change. It is also an example of the use of indirect and soft intellectual "smart" power as opposed to direct and brutal physical power.

All this is nothing radical or new. The too often berated Niccolo Machiavelli had it right. Successful interstate and intrastate conflict must be fought with *prudenza* (i.e., prudence, moral rectitude, self-restraint, and justice). In this way, a belligerent can strongly influence the kind of security and peace that one would like to achieve over the long term.[30]

CHAPTER 2

Stability—or Not: Lessons from Italy (1968–1983) and Western Sahara (1975–Present)

This chapter discusses the critical nature of stability in dealing with state and nonstate actors within the context of the security concept and the national and global security arena. The main themes emphasize the following: (1) the relationship of stability to security, (2) stability as a key element in the "new" peace-security equation, (3) the threat to national and/or international security if ignored or misused, and (4) this chapter provides two accompanying vignettes.

The first vignette is a positive example from which to learn how a government might defeat an insurgency. The example is that of the Red Brigades' failed attempt to attack and destroy the stability of the "moribund Italian state"—and the state's response. The second vignette provides a certain negative balance. It is the story of an ongoing asymmetric program that has created a humanitarian disaster in the northwest African territory that was once called Spanish or Western Sahara.

Probably, the most important lesson here is that contemporary attempts to either destroy or maintain the stability of any given actor in the global security arena are keys to the national and international security. The results of either aggressive or defensive actions are no longer determined by means of well-equipped and easily identified military forces. At base, the most effective player in the security arena has now become the political actor who plans and implements the multidimensional kinds of indirect and direct, nonmilitary and military, and nonlethal and lethal internal and external activities that threaten or defend a given society's general well-being and exploit the root causes of internal instability. Consequently, the most effective threats to national and/or global stability are not necessarily direct attacks on a government. Indirect attacks, however, are proven means for weakening governing regimes. These "new" threats reflect a logical progression from the problems of state weaknesses and, in turn, move the threat spectrum from traditional nation-state to nontraditional nonstate actors and unconventional methods.[1] Thus, the primary and specific effort that ultimately defeats or defends a given political-economic-social system and forces radial political-economic-social change is the multidimensional erosion or strengthening of a people's morale and the political will of its leadership. The better a protagonist is at conducting this persuasive-coercive, stability-instability effort, the more effective that protagonist will be relative to the opposition. Accordingly, as Clausewitz taught, the contemporary primary center of gravity changes from a familiar military concept to a complex and ambiguous leadership and public opinion paradigm.[2]

THE RELATIONSHIP OF STABILITY TO SECURITY

Some International Legal Background

In the past, sovereignty was the unquestioned control of territory and the people in it. Sovereignty is now conditional. It goes beyond the control of people to the responsibility to generate the stability that enables development, democracy, and sustainable peace for a people (i.e., responsible governance). At the same time, sovereignty (i.e., security) has become the responsibility to protect and prevent a people from egregious harm. The international legal protection and prevention principles have also taken on new meanings. For example, in addition to traditional nation-state aggression, the list of external and internal threats to stability and security now include malgovernance, attacks on cybersecurity, natural and human-made disasters, health risks, environmental issues, the global drug trafficking, trafficking in persons, and virtually all the ever-present root causes of instability.[3]

As it has been mentioned earlier, all this works two ways. First, stability is required to effectively protect and/or prevent a coerced transition of the values of a given society. Second, stability is the critical element in the security equation that a given aggressor must attack successfully in order to force an enemy to accede to his or her radical political-economic-social demands. This forced transition of values poses an existential threat to national and international security and defines war. Thus, security ultimately depends on the eradication of the causes as well as the perpetrators of instability.[4]

Lastly, it is important to remember that in the anarchy of international politics, enforcement of the international law concepts of sovereignty and protective and preventative defense against aggression has tended to be undertaken only by the major powers of the day. They have done this using their own power unilaterally, in concert with allies, proxies, and/or in accordance with relevant protocols, agreements, accords, conventions, declarations, resolutions, and treaties. International organizations such as the United Nations, the Organization of American States, the Permanent Court of Arbitration, and other international bodies, however, have no effective means for enforcing their resolutions and statements of opinion.

STABILITY AS A KEY ELEMENT IN THE PEACE-SECURITY EQUATION

Security and Stability

Security begins with the provision of personal protection to individual members of the citizenry (e.g., stability). It extends to protection of the collectivity from violent internal nonstate actors and repressive malgovernance. It also extends to aggressive nation-state adversaries—that is, individual and collective stability. That stability is dependent on a governing regime that can and will create and enforce the rule of law. The legitimate rule of law enables the internal and individual order that, in turn, enables the state to develop internal socioeconomic-political infrastructure. That infrastructure enables the state to develop national and regional non-kinetic and kinetic power and a higher level of personal and collective security. The resultant stability leads around and around to peace and security again and again. At the same time, it spirals and circles back again and again to higher levels of stability and security—or not—that is, the phenomenon moves upward when used positively and downward when used negatively.

Security, then, depends on the positive upward expansion of the socioeconomic-political infrastructure that can only be generated through stability. These measures provide for the generation of technical, professional, and ethical bases from which competent political leadership can provide greater and better individual and collective well-being. Unless and until a people perceive that every program, policy, and action taken against a given internal or external adversary contributes directly toward enhancing its perception that governmental authority serves the popular need and is applied in a morally correct manner, the government will find itself in a negative crisis of governance—that is, a governing regime will likely face increasing social violence, criminal anarchy, terrorism, insurgency, and the potential for being deposed.[5]

The Security-Peace Paradigm

The security-peace paradigm outlined in Chapter 1 summarizes the basic circular linkage and relevance of the highly interrelated components of the peace-security concept. Again, they are as follows: (1) military/police (M) capability to provide personal and collective stability (i.e., well-being); (2) economic (E) ability to generate long-term socioeconomic-political development; and (3) political capability (PC) to develop the type of responsible governance to which a given polity can relate and support. That takes us back to security and stability. That is: Security $(S) = M + E \times PC$. Importantly, this linkage can be used positively (i.e., constructively) or negatively (i.e., destructively). Thus, this equation can be used to create stability or instability, development or stagnation, prosperity or poverty, responsible governance or malgovernance, or peace and security, or conflict and instability.

This circular pattern seems to take us around and around, again and again. To be more than temporarily effective, however, the peace-security equation requires the development of an upward positive spiral. Otherwise, with no improvement in personal and collective well-being and relatively no socioeconomic-political development, a situation is created that would be, in fact, a downward and negative movement toward state failure and its aftermath. In sum, and as noted previously, stability is the foundational element that enables socioeconomic-political development and peace and security.[6]

THE THREAT TO NATIONAL AND GLOBAL SECURITY

The Quintuple Threat

The issues and problems noted earlier represent a quintuple threat to the authority, legitimacy, and stability of targeted governments. As a consequence, this threat takes us to the larger threat of state failure. The state failure, however, is not the ultimate threat. The ultimate threat is that of the aftermath of state failure.

Generally, the quintuple set of threats outlines a negative destabilization process. It includes the following: (1) undermining the ability of a government to perform its legitimizing functions; (2) significantly changing a government's foreign, defense, and other policies; (3) isolating religious or racial communities from the rest of a host nation's society and replacing traditional state authority with alternative governance (e.g., ideological, plutocratic, criminal, or religious); (4) transforming socially isolated human terrain into "virtual states" within the host state, without a centralized bureaucracy or easily identified military or police forces; and (5) conducting low-cost actions calculated to maximize damage, minimize response, and display carefully staged media events that lead to the erosion of the legitimacy and stability of a targeted state's political-economic-social system.

The Ultimate Threat

Somewhere near the end of the destabilization process, the state will be able to control less of its national territory and fewer people in it. Nevertheless, just because a state fails does not mean that it will go away. The diminishment of responsible governance and personal security generates greater poverty, violence, and instability—and a downward spiral in terms of development and well-being. It is a zero-sum game in which nonstate or individual actors (e.g., insurgents, transnational criminal organizations, and corrupt public officials) are the winners and the rest of the society is the loser. Ultimately, failing or failed states become dysfunctional states, dependencies, tribal states, rogue states, criminal states, narco-states, new "peoples' republics," draconian states (e.g., military dictatorships), neo-populist states (e.g., civilian dictatorships), or just disappear from the face of the earth. Moreover, failing or failed states may possibly dissolve and become parts of other states or may reconfigure into entirely new good or bad entities. In that context, however, Boutros Boutros-Ghali would remind us that the ultimate threat is that of the unwelcome radical imposition of the winner's values on the loser.[7]

VIGNETTE 1: REFLECTIONS ON THE ITALIAN EXPERIENCE AGAINST THE RED BRIGADES, 1968–1983

Introduction

In post–Napoleonic Europe, Italy was defined simply as a geographic expression. In post–World War II Europe, Italy had only advanced to the status of "the sick man of Europe." That "sick" country was experiencing virtually every symptom of a failing state status. Productivity, as well as gross domestic product (GDP), was down. The Italian currency was down and moving further downward. The only statistics moving upward on the charts were labor strife, poverty, crime, and emigration. In that socioeconomic milieu, chronic political instability was illustrated by the succession of 39 governments over 35 years between the promulgation of the 1948 Constitution and 1983. This state of affairs adversely affected societal relations and increased Italy's vulnerability to criminal and subversive designs. As a result, from 1968 to 1983, over 300 different "leftist" groups (i.e., the Red Brigades), along with several additional militant separatist, pacifist, anarchist, and monarchist organizations, mobilized and conducted a terrorism strategy to overthrow the "moribund Italian state." The so-called Red Brigades were at the forefront of that campaign and proved to be the most practical, calculative, and cynical of all the Italian "terrorist" organizations conducing a terrorist-political-psychological war against the stability of the state.[8]

Additional Context

Italian "terrorism" was not taken very seriously from the 1960s through the 1970s and was allowed to fester and grow. Not until after the highly publicized peoples' trial and execution of the very popular five-time prime minister, Aldo Moro, did the Italian government directly address the issue of instability and violence. The murder of Prime Minister Moro marked the first time in more than 10 years of kidnapping, murder, maiming, and bombing, so the Italian government decided that the violent actions of the various antigovernment organizations constituted more than a complex social and law enforcement problem. These various organizations, or gang equivalents, were challenging the integrity of the country's political institutions and creating an unacceptable level of internal instability. Decision makers began to understand that the intent of every 1 of the 300 or more leftist, rightist, and separatist antigovernment organizations, led by the Red Brigades, was to destroy the political equilibrium of the Italian state and force radical political-economic-social change. It was not until then that the increasing violence, criminality, and threat to the state were finally recognized as a serious national security problem.[9]

Findings

The program of the Red Brigades was straightforward, transparent, and unchanged from the organization's beginnings in 1960 through the early 1980s. The leadership stressed terrorism as a tactic and an operational-level strategy in an unconventional urban guerrilla war. Leaders assumed that terrorism would challenge the integrity of Italy's political and socio-economic institutions and create an unacceptable level of instability. In turn, the resultant instability was expected to erode the basic public trust that must underlie the legitimate functioning of the state. That, in turn, would lead to the geostrategic objective of changing the Italian political-economic-social structure to something dictated by the leadership of the Red Brigades (i.e., the dictatorship of the proletariat).[10]

Response

Thus, after 8–10 years of instability and the assassination of Moro, the Italian government began to realize that its unwillingness to consider the Red Brigades as more than a social and law enforcement problem could lead to the destruction of the state. The government also began to understand that it must develop a long-term, multidimensional, and morally acceptable strategy to confront the various violent internal non-state actors who were threatening the stability, sovereignty, and security of the country. In these terms, like it or not, the government had a clear responsibility to take legitimate measures to confront the Red Brigades and avoid the intended destruction of the state. Once the government made the political decision to treat the increasing levels of violence and instability generated by the Red Brigades as a national security problem, it began to plan, organize, and implement a multidimensional paramilitary people-centric response. However, because of the continuing absence of a homogeneous parliamentary majority and the resultant political instability, the government could not micromanage the paradigm. Fortunately for Italy, the government was limited to the promulgation of fundamental measures that would facilitate the conduct of a counterterrorist strategy at the national security level.

Accordingly, the parliament did what it could and should. It passed legislation that would bring the criminal code up to date and allow the legitimate prosecution of a serious antiterrorist war. The parliament also provided sociopolitical-economic programs and reforms designed to directly preempt the militants' terrorism strategy of attacking the "moribund Italian state." At the same time, the parliament gave the overall planning and coordination of the national security challenge to the relatively well-respected paramilitary *Carabinieri*. The regular Italian military would not be involved in an antiterrorist war.[11]

The mandate given to the various security instruments of the state that would implement the counterterrorism effort was threefold. First, the various sociopolitical-economic-paramilitary security instruments of the Italian state would integrate all counterterrorist actions under the direction of a *Carabinieri* general (i.e., General Carlo Alberto Dalla Chiesa)—that is, there would be a complete unity of effort. Second, together these unifying and legitimizing efforts would reestablish the kind of stability that is derived from popular Italian perceptions that the authority of the state was genuine and effective and it used morally correct means for reasonable and fair purposes—that is, the geostrategic objective of the effort would be to reestablish and enhance the legitimacy of the state. Third, there would be no "dirty war." In short, unity of effort and prudence would generate the stability necessary to develop a state of prosperity and peace in Italy.[12]

The application of this paradigm would result in a multidimensional, population-centric, and geostrategic effort involving a series of highly interrelated wars within the general antiterrorist conflict. Those wars would include the following: (1) a more-or-less conventional paramilitary law-enforcement "war" against the various terrorist organizations; (2) a strong effort (i.e., "war") to guarantee the morally prudent use of that force; (3) a "war" to unify a multidimensional effort within the Italian bureaucracy and the *Carabinieri*; (4) an information "war" to convince the Italian people of the moral rectitude of the counterterrorist campaign;

(5) a "war" to isolate the various militant organizations from their internal and external support; (6) an intelligence "war" to locate and neutralize the men and women who lead, plan, and execute terrorist actions; and (7) a "war" for legitimacy and the moral right of the incumbent democratically elected regime to exist. These are the primary means through which a government may be attacked and destroyed. On the other side of the proverbial coin, these are also the means by which a government may attack an adversary's strategy and/or defend itself.

The keys to success encompassed in the "wars within the war" of the Italian experience included the following: (1) a realistic, strategic vision to counter the unconventional challenge to the state; (2) a management structure to plan, unify, and implement that vision; and (3) the prudent use of appropriate political-economic-social-security instruments of state to conduct the multidimensional wars within the general war.[13]

Outcome

The Italian experience with urban irregular war was the transition point toward a new age of unconventional conflict in which the definition of "enemy" became elusive and the use of "power" against that adversary became diffuse. Underlying these ambiguous issues was that this war was an intrastate affair—it was Italians versus Italians, not nation-state versus nation-state. All these ambiguities intruded on the traditional Italian and world vision of war and required a new paradigm that would address the addition of several political-social-psychological-moral dimensions designed to attack the strategy of the Italian Red Brigade phenomenon. *Carabinieri* general Dalla Chiesa got it right. He had studied Clausewitz, Vladimir Ilyich Lenin, Niccolo Machiavelli, and Sun Tzu. He knew what to do and how to do it.

In the more conventional paramilitary war, the *Carabinieri* gained the approval of the Italian polity and contributed directly to the enhancement of the popular perception that paramilitary action was used discreetly and for reasonable and legitimate purposes. That, in turn, generated positive implications for future social peace in Italy. Under General Dalla Chiesa's leadership, long-term and short-term mutually supportive objectives were determined and pursued and the Red Brigades were brought under control as early as 1981–1982.[14]

In the war for unity of effort, the Italian government understood that lack of *unison* (unity of effort) was a major deficiency in the conduct of the business of the state and the antiterrorist campaign. As noted earlier, the parliament passed an emergency national security measure that created a temporary task force composed of state police, the finance guard, and *Carabinieri* personnel. As a consequence, planning and coordination, to the extent that it was achieved in Italy, essentially fell to that task force.

Although not perfect or all-encompassing, it proved to be adequate to the task at hand, achieved most of its objectives, and was a vitally important element in the process of neutralizing the Red Brigades and their allies.[15]

In the information war, the state and the media embarked on a strong counterterrorist, public diplomacy campaign. The objectives were to expose and exploit the fact that the various left-wing, right-wing, separatist, monarchist, and other groups making up the Red Brigade phenomenon were not popular organizations representing the Italian masses. Rather, these groups were self-appointed elites whose goals were not in line with what the people wanted or needed. In the final analysis, the government's antiterrorist information "war" demonstrated that as far as the terrorists were concerned, Italians who were not ideologically "true believers" were not really people. As an example, the 2,384 victims who had been murdered, maimed, or kidnapped by any one of the various terrorist groups in 1979 were not considered to be human beings deserving of personal dignity. Instead, these victims were considered to be "tools of the system," "pigs," and "watch dogs." Moreover, the court trials of the terrorists revealed that the Red Brigades considered everyone else—even comrades on the left—to be mere "shit." As a result, terrorist violence began to be increasingly perceived by the Italian public as wanton and well beyond what might be necessary to make a political statement.[16]

In the intelligence war, the short-term effect was to neutralize a given terrorist group. The long-term effect was to shift the balance of power decidedly toward the legitimate organs of the Italian state. A specific example of this situation is instructive. Because of the self-imposed protective isolation of the Italian terrorist organizations, they had only little intelligence with which they had to work. In stark contrast, the state developed a large and increasingly effective intelligence network. Nevertheless, the role played by the legal Italian Communist Party (PCI) was probably the most interesting and decisive factor in destroying the Red Brigades and their various allies. The PCI's capillary structure was able to identify and locate specific organizations, leaders, and members relatively easily and quickly. The PCI furnished a great deal of this information/intelligence to the state security organizations and made them look to be much more efficient and effective than they really were. In any event, timely and accurate human intelligence provided by the PCI significantly enhanced the Italian government's ability to attack and defeat the Red Brigades.[17]

In the war to isolate the terrorists from their sources of support, the *Carabinieri* was able to isolate politically, economically, psychologically, and militarily the violent irregular and asymmetric opposition from their primary sources of aid. Internally, the Italian gang phenomenon was isolated from the rest of the society as a result of the effects of the legitimacy war, the information war, and the police-paramilitary war. As the terrorists withdrew more into their highly secretive and compartmental-ized organizational structure, they isolated themselves from the rest of the Italian community. That separation restricted access to external as well as internal support, the capability to recruit new members, and the ability to organize significant actions.[18]

In the legitimacy war, once the Italian parliament had provided the legislation that would allow the prosecution of a serious antiterrorism war, legitimacy was recognized as key to the success or failure of the ter-rorist gang phenomenon—or for the government. The Red Brigades, for example, identified legitimacy as the primary center of gravity in their strategy to destroy the incumbent regime. The Italian bureaucracy under-stood that popular perceptions of various injustices tended to limit the right—and the ability—of the government to conduct the business of the state. It countered with programs designed to preempt the militants' anti-government terrorism strategy. As noted elsewhere, that task was to ensure that every policy, program, and action—political, economic, social, opinion making, and security—would contribute directly toward enhanc-ing the popular perception that governmental authority did, in fact, serve public needs and was applied in a morally correct manner.[19]

Implications and Conclusion

In the late 1970s and early 1980s, the Italians and the rest of the world began to realize that terrorism was likely to be the most important national and international political phenomenon of the twenty-first century. Decision makers, policy makers, opinion makers, and administrators began to realize that the terrorist threat was caused, exacerbated, and allowed to intensify because the elected institutions of government failed to provide responsible governance. This kind of threat is different in nature and method from that of the past unconventional conflicts. In the past, the enemy was a clearly dis-cernible military force, backed by a nation-state's industrial capability to cre-ate and then maintain that military force outside its own borders. Now, the enemy is not a traditional, recognizable military entity with a "fixed address" and clearly defined traditional military maneuver methods. Rather, the enemy now becomes an elusive state, nonstate, or individual political actor who utilizes indirect, nonkinetic, and ambiguous confronta-tional methods. This new kind of confrontation cannot be dealt successfully with infantry, tanks, and aircraft attacking specific territory or destroying buildings, neighborhoods, or cities. More than anything else, strategic suc-cess in contemporary conflict is based on sophisticated political-psychological "smart" nonkinetic power directed at influencing public opinion in one's favor. All this calls for a "new" paradigm.

The Italian case demonstrates that success in countering terrorism and asymmetric war in the "new world disorder" will be constructed on the same theoretical bases that supported favorable results in the past. Even though every conflict is situation specific, it is not unique. Throughout the universe of possibilities, there are analytical commonalities at the strategic and high operational levels. In particular, the seven dimensions, or dependent variables, noted in the preceding Outcome section determine the success or failure of an asymmetric, irregular intrastate conflict. The paradigm illustrated in this Italian case (and others) has power and virtue in part because of the symmetry of its application to a besieged government and its allies and to a violent internal challenger and its allies—that is to say, no successful strategy on either side of the conflict spectrum has been formulated over the past 50–60 years that has not explicitly or implicitly taken into account the strategic dimensions, or "wars within the war," as applied in this Italian case.[20]

The Italian experience with the Red Brigades illustrates the proven "best practices" through which to reverse the impetus toward coerced radical political-economic-social change or failed state status. This strategy dismantled the Red Brigades within a short two- to three-year period and with very little collateral damage to the Italian population.[21]

KEY POINTS AND LESSONS

Key Points

- The international legal protection and prevention principles have taken on new meaning. For example, in addition to traditional nation-state aggression, the list of external and internal threats to stability/security now include malgovernance, attacks on cybersecurity, natural and human-made disasters, health risks, environmental issues, global drug trafficking, trafficking in persons, and virtually all the ever-present root causes of instability.

- Security depends on the continued and expanded building of the socioeconomic-political infrastructure that can only be generated by stability. These measures also provide for the generation of technical, professional, and ethical bases from which competent political leadership can provide individual and collective well-being. That, in turn, enables the state to develop national and regional nonkinetic and kinetic power, personal and collective stability, and internal and external peace.

- The issues and problems noted earlier represent serious threats to the authority, legitimacy, and stability of targeted governments. These threats take us to the larger threat of state failure. The state failure, however, is not the ultimate threat. Once again, the ultimate threat is the aftermath of state failure.

- The challenge, then, is to come to terms with the fact that contemporary security, at whatever level, is at base a holistic political-diplomatic, socioeconomic, psychological-moral, and military-police effort. The corollary is to change from a singular military or law enforcement approach to a multidimensional, multi-organizational, multicultural, and multinational paradigm.

- The Italian government, once it made the political decision to treat the increasing levels of violence and instability generated by the Red Brigades as a national security problem, planned, organized, and implemented a prudent and relatively soft multilayered political-paramilitary response. That approach toward attacking the militants' strategy was successful and brought terrorism under control within a surprisingly short period of time.

Lessons

The current threat from the protean asymmetric insurgency phenomenon (i.e., unconventional political-military, socioeconomic, and psychological-moral war) is different in nature and method from that of many past conflicts. In the past, what mattered most were military bases, preserving access to sea lines of communication, choke points, raw materials, and territory—and denying those assets to one's nation-state enemies. And, in the past, the enemy was a clearly discernible military or insurgent force backed by a nation-state's industrial capability to create and maintain a viable force outside its own frontiers. Now, adversaries tend to utilize unconventional and indirect confrontational methods to coerce radical political-economic-social change in a given polity and/or society.

General Rupert Smith reminds us that "We are now engaged constantly and in many permutations, in wars amongst the people. We must adapt our approaches and organize our institutions to this overwhelming reality if we are to triumph in the confrontations and conflicts that we face."[22] This is an indispensable lesson from the Italian experience with the terrorist Red Brigades.

VIGNETTE 2: THE HUMANITARIAN DISASTER IN WESTERN SAHARA

Introduction

The modern Western Sahara, previously known as the Spanish Sahara, *Rio de Oro*, and/or the Sahrawi Arab Republic (SADR), is a generally desert territory in northwest Africa located along the Atlantic coast between Morocco, Algeria, and Mauritania. It is relatively sparsely populated, is rich in phosphate and iron ore, enjoys a profitable fishing industry, and is believed to hold significant oil deposits. Western Sahara is also the location of a nearly 70-year-long dispute between Spain, France, Morocco, Algeria, Mauritania, and the local Sahrawi people. The current dispute centers on the issue of Moroccan political-military control of the area on one side of the proverbial coin and the political independence of the Sahrawi people on the other.[23]

The Issue and Context

In the summer and fall of 1975, several deciding events began to take place that have kept the region in a state of tension and turmoil for the past 40 or more years. Spain entered negotiations with Morocco and Mauritania that led to the tripartite Madrid Accords that would transfer parts of Spanish Sahara to both those countries. The Sahrawi people were not a party to those discussions. That led POLISARIO (i.e., the insurgent Sahrawi military organization) and SADR (i.e., the political organization intended to act as the sovereign representative of the Sahrawi people) to violently oppose those accords.[24]

Findings and Response

Morocco asked the International Court of Justice (ICJ) to offer its opinion regarding Moroccan claims to Spanish Sahara. On October 16, 1975, the court found that Spanish Sahara's historical ties to Morocco and Mauritania did not grant those countries the right to that territory. To add insult to Moroccan injury, the court also declared that the Sahrawi people, as the true owners of the land, held a right of self-determination. Thus, any solution to the issue of integration with, or independence from, any other country required the explicit approval of the Sahrawi people. Neither Morocco nor Mauritania accepted the decision of the ICJ.

On November 6, 1975, King Hassan II of Morocco announced that he would organize and lead a "Green March" to "reclaim" the Western Sahara. That extremely innovative well-planned and well-executed effort mobilized 300,000–350,000 unarmed men, women, and children who would cross into Western Sahara to claim the territory as a part of "Greater Morocco." Spanish security forces were ordered *not* to resist the flood of unarmed civilians. The march continued for four days, by which time the marchers had pushed approximately 10 km into Spanish Sahara. At that point, King Hassan II halted the march and allowed his "volunteers" to return to Morocco. On November 14, with the Moroccans back home and no one hurt, Spain, Morocco, and Mauritania signed the accords that set out the terms for the transfer of power in the region from Spain to Morocco and Mauritania. The three counties were given joint control over the territory until 1976 when Spain would leave the Western Sahara entirely. At that point, Morocco would annex the northern two-thirds of Spanish Sahara and Mauritania would take control of the southern one-third of the former Spanish province.

Algerian support to POLISARIO provided the resources that allowed that organization to attack Mauritanian targets. Direct attacks on those targets resulted in a *coup d'etat* that brought a new Mauritanian government to power, the withdrawal of Mauritanian troops from

Western Sahara, and recognition of SADR as the sovereign government in the former Spanish Sahara. The celebration of that POLISARIO victory, however, was short-lived. Almost immediately after the Mauritanian troops had left their one-third of the territory, Morocco annexed the area. Thus, POLISARIO and SADR were forced to cease acting as security and political institutions of a nation-state and went back to the role of proxy nonstate insurgent actors, totally dependent on Algeria.[25]

Outcome

Algerian support to POLISARIO precipitated the need for Morocco to build, defend, and maintain a costly 1,500 km berm (the Moroccan Wall) that separates the commercially profitable parts of Moroccan-controlled Western Sahara from the almost uninhabited and unproductive remainder of what used to be Spanish Sahara. Thus, POLISARIO controls the small, generally unproductive territory east of the Moroccan Wall, and Algeria houses the majority of the Sahrawi people.

Protests, demonstrations, parades, conferences, sporadic fighting, and the UN peacekeeping effort have continued off and on over the past several years. The United Nations authorized a mission (MINURSO) to make arrangements for a referendum and to preclude a resumption of armed conflict in the area. That referendum has not taken place, but peace has been maintained. The sticking point, not surprisingly, is that Morocco insists that Moroccan citizens who have settled in Western Sahara since 1975—and who now make up a majority of the population—be allowed to vote in the referendum.

In March 2016, the secretary general of the United Nations, Ban Ki-moon, visited Sahrawi refugee camps in Algeria. On that occasion, he described Western Sahara as being "occupied." The Moroccan reaction was virtually immediate and hostile. Morocco ordered the UN MINURSO mission to close down and leave within 72 hours. The United Nations complied. Subsequently, the Security Council asked Morocco to allow the reopening of the mission and resumption of the full MINURSO mandate. Morocco agreed and the situation reverted back to the status quo ante. As of this writing, no one expects much of anything to change anytime soon.[26]

The stark realities are as follows: (1) Morocco exercises de facto sovereignty in Western Sahara and enjoys the legitimacy that comes from the barrel of a gun being held out of sight; (2) Morocco is firmly in control of Western Sahara and shows no inclination to change its position here; (3) without serious support from the major world powers, the United Nations has no way to enforce international court decisions or other forms of international law; and (4) if you are a teenager, one of the very few career paths available is that of an Islamic "fighter."

Implications and Conclusions

This vignette provides a clear-cut example of the ultimate security threat. As noted earlier, that threat is not instability or even state failure. What has taken place in the territory that was once called Spanish Sahara and/or Western Sahara is a humanitarian disaster that is the sum and substance of the aftermath of contemporary conflict and state failure. What has also taken place is a good example of the operational result of intelligently and slowly attacking the stability of a given territory and people in it. The final political geostrategic result of the exercise is expected to be the creation of a "Greater Morocco."

In this "new" security environment, war is no longer an exclusive military-diplomatic undertaking conducted by traditional nation-states. The power to make war, control war, and destroy states and societies is now within the reach of virtually anyone or any organization with a "cause." Combatants are not necessarily military units. They tend to be groups of individuals that are not necessarily uniformed, not necessarily male but also female, and not necessarily adults but also children. Combatants may also be proxies for players who wish to maintain the international legal fiction of "plausible deniability." Traditional and nontraditional actors must, more often than not, deal with the absence of a credible government or political actor with which to negotiate and the lack of a guarantee that any agreement between or among contending players will be honored. Nevertheless, war—declared or undeclared, or whatever "spin doctors" might call it—remains an act of coercion to compel an adversary to do one's will. Once again, there are the following three rules: (1) traditional rules of war are not enforceable, (2) only the foolish fight fair, and (3) promoting or protecting national self-interests is the only morality. Accordingly, war is not limited; it is unrestricted.[27]

KEY POINTS AND LESSONS

Key Points

- Contemporary conflict is not just a test of expertise creating instability, conducting relatively bloodless violence (e.g., the Green March), or achieving some sort of visceral satisfaction. Instead, for aggressors and defenders alike, it is an exercise of survival in an anarchical world. Failure is not an option.

- Conflict—declared or undeclared, violent or benign, or whatever it may be called—remains an act of coercion to compel an adversary to do one's will.

- Without serious support from the major world powers, the United Nations, the ICJ, and other international organizations have no way to enforce their resolutions, decisions, or other instruments of international law.

- This vignette provides a clear-cut example of the ultimate security threat. What has taken place in Western Sahara is a humanitarian disaster that is the result of a purposeful Moroccan strategy designed to destroy the SADR and create a "Greater Morocco."

- On the other hand, what Morocco has achieved in Western Sahara is a classic case study in the superiority of a well-planned and carefully executed combination of nonkinetic and kinetic ways and means to slowly, but surely, compel an adversary to acquiesce to one's will.

Lessons

At base, the most effective player in the contemporary security arena has become the political actor who (1) carefully plans and implements the multidimensional kinds of indirect and direct, nonmilitary and military, and nonlethal internal and external activities; (2) threatens or defends a given societies' general well-being; and (3) exploits the root causes of internal instability. The better a protagonist is at conducting this persuasive-coercive stability-instability effort, the more effective that protagonist will be relative to the opposition. Accordingly, as Clausewitz taught over 200 years ago, the contemporary center of gravity changes from a familiar military-centric concept to a complex and ambiguous leadership and national and international public opinion paradigm.[28] In that context, Sun Tzu could have reminded us 2,500 years ago that there are more effective ways to attack an enemy's strategy than conventional military-centric wars of attrition. "To win one hundred victories in one hundred battles is not the acme of skill. To subdue the enemy without fighting is the acme of skill."[29]

CHAPTER 3

Stability and Security: Lessons That Should Have Been Learned in Somalia (1992–1993) and the British and American Experience in Bosnia (1992–1998)

As emphasized throughout this book, security and stability begin with the provision of personal protection and well-being of individual members of a polity. That, then, extends to protection of the collectivity from violent external nonstate and state enemies. That is a definition of stability. Personal and collective protection and well-being enables socioeconomic-political development. At the same time, personal and collective security has a decisive bearing on establishing and maintaining internal order, enhancing national well-being, and strengthening legitimate governance and, therefore, also enables internal and external peace. That is a definition of security. The reasoning is straightforward. Personal and collective well-being (i.e., stability) is the foundational cornerstone for building a country's socioeconomic-political infrastructure and the capability to sustain a durable peace.

Consequently, we discuss the following: (1) the idea of personal and collective protection of a polity and (2) three keys that provide the means to go beyond simple protection of socioeconomic-political development. They are the national development, the end-state planning process, and the creation of strategic clarity (i.e., unity of effort). Again, the accompanying vignettes are examples of how *not* to go about the process of achieving stability and the desired security. An examination of the Somalia case, 1992–1993, fairly screams of a doomed attempt to provide the stable environment and the planning process needed to move on toward a sustainable peace. Additionally, as noted earlier, we provide another very interesting example of how *not* to go about achieving stability—that is, the case of Bosnia, 1992–1998. The consistency of the lessons learned from these and similar cases warrants confidence that these strategic-level lessons take into account the major unifying dimensions of effective peace efforts and should begin the process of rethinking both problem and response in a world of dangerous uncertainty and ambiguity.

PERSONAL AND COLLECTIVE PROTECTION OF A POLITY

Stability encompasses several ideas noted in the previous chapters. At a minimum, the three components of stability that must be developed are as follows: (1) the military-police capability to provide an acceptable level of internal and external safety; (2) the socioeconomic capacity to generate real safety and political development; and (3) the political competence to develop a type of governance to which a given society can relate and support, that is, sustainable peace. That also is a part of the definition of security. Classical development theory generally emphasizes the idea that economic development automatically creates sociopolitical development.[1] That is not what has happened. The result has been a significant distortion of the real relationship among the closely related components of stability and security.

Several high-ranking civilian and military officials have explained their lack of success in relatively recent conflict resolution episodes as the result of little, no, or inadequate guidance from their political masters. What seemed to matter was that their actions appeared to be operational actions doing "something." This reminds one of Alice's conversations with the Cheshire cat in *Alice's Adventures in Wonderland*. Alice asked, "Would you tell me please, which way I ought to go from here?" "That depends a good deal on where you want to get to," said the cat. "I don't much care where . . ." said Alice. "Then it doesn't matter which way you go," said the cat, "so long as I get somewhere," Alice added as an explanation. "Oh, you're sure to do that," said the cat, "if you only walk long enough."[2]

There is a calculus suggested in this logic. The idea is that strategies succeed or fail depending on whether there is, in fact, a strategy. There must also be an end-state planning process and a cooperative implementation methodology (i.e., strategic clarity) that can place the strategic geopolitical end state on a durable foundation. Otherwise, it will be only a matter of time before a lapse into instability and internal conflict occurs. That also underlines the importance of our so-called war for unity of effort.

THREE KEYS THAT PROVIDE THE MEANS TO GO BEYOND SIMPLE PROTECTION TO SOCIOECONOMIC-POLITICAL DEVELOPMENT

The reality of the situation is that stability, national development, and security result from the complex interplay of the three components identified in Chapter 1 and outlined later. Each is essential to achieve long-term stability and to generate the capability to sustain a durable foundation for peace. Even though security/military/economic components can be developed independent of each other, the political competence component is the one that holds everything together. That is: $S = M + E \times PC$. The fulfillment of this holistic responsible governance and security-peace paradigm consists of these three principal elements. They are conceptual and operational. First, the national development $(M + E)$ requires a rethinking and restructuring of the stability concept. The second is end-state planning. The third recognizes that development and planning are necessary but not sufficient to achieve a geopolitical end state. There are two more requirements here. First, there must be an organization adequate to the task. Second, there must also be appropriately educated personnel willing to work together to achieve a common geopolitical objective (PC). That is a definition of strategic clarity. The simplest definition of strategic clarity, however, is a complete unity of effort.[3]

National Development

Over the years, the international security dialogue has focused on national development as the key element in the security equation. The generally uncoordinated, piecemeal, ad hoc, and military-centric approach to socioeconomic-political development has not proven adequate to the task. Strong empirical evidence demonstrates that unless solutions to development problems are addressed on a coherent, long-term, legitimizing, and people-centric basis, no self-sustaining national development can take place. On the other hand, a holistic people-centric paradigm for national development provides the bases from which the nation-state can develop the political and economic strength to generate internal order and socioeconomic-political progress. At the same time, a viable national development paradigm would provide the foundational capability to protect and enhance the interests of the state at home and in the international security arena. Thus, a self-sustaining and holistic national development approach to national and personal well-being provides stability and makes a significant contribution to security.[4] The key to the implementation of a viable political stability strategy and strategic clarity is planning. This depends on a clear strategic vision based on the populace-oriented model as a starting point. This takes us to a more complete discussion of end-state planning and strategic clarity.

End-State Planning

End-state planning starts with the truism that conflict is a continuation of politics by other means but with two qualifying arguments. First, military/police violence is required only when the conditions or changes sought cannot be achieved through political-diplomatic, socioeconomic, or informational-psychological ways and means. Second, end-state planning advocates synchronization of all national and international nonkinetic and kinetic instruments of power so that the most synergism can be gained from the interaction of the variables selected for action.[5] The end-state planning argument concludes that if the United Nations or the United States or any other international player is going to succeed in future conflicts, civil and military forces must be structured and employed in ways that respond to the dynamic political, economic, social, and military variables at work within the security-peace paradigm. Additionally, and most importantly, logic and empirical experience demand that the interagency community must base its decisions on a clear, mutually agreed upon definition of what ultimate success looks like—that is, again, share a common vision of the geostrategic end state. The requirement for a high level of planning and coordination is not a matter of just going "somewhere." It is a matter of knowing where you are going and precisely how you are going to get there.[6]

Strategic Clarity

The lessons from a half-century of bitter experience suffered by governments involved in dealing with internal and global instabilities and destabilizers show that a given internal or external intervention often ends short of achieving the mandated peace. Too often, this is because short-, mid-, and long-term objectives are unclear; the endgame is undefined; consistent and appropriate support is not provided; and civil-military unity of purpose remains unachieved. Thus, it is imperative to develop leaders, policy makers, implementers, and organizational structures that can generate strategic clarity and make it work. It must be remembered that the final outcome of conflicts such as those in Algeria, Italy, Malaya, Portugal, and Vietnam was not determined by the skillful manipulation of violence on the battlefield. Rather, control of the situation and its resolution were determined by the qualitative leader judgments, and the synergistic processes (i.e., planning for unity of effort) established before, during, and after a conflict were politically recognized to have begun and ended. These are the essential components of strategic clarity and to success in the new millennium.[7]

CONCLUSIONS: TOWARD SECURITY AND PEACE

Analysis of the problems of legitimate governance and stability with justice (i.e., security and peace) takes us beyond providing some form of humanitarian assistance or refugee assistance in cases of human misery and need. It also takes us beyond the traditional monitoring of bilateral agreements or protecting one group of people from another or from a state or nonstate actor. It also takes us beyond compelling one or more parties to a conflict to cease human rights violations and other morally repugnant activities and beyond repelling simple aggression. Analysis of the problems of governance and stability takes us back to where we began.

The core strategic problem is the responsible political leadership (i.e., responsible sovereignty) in the post–Cold War world. Foreign policy and military asset management must sooner or later address this central issue. The enormity and logic of the establishment of a durable and just peace demand the following: (1) a well-defined, mutually agreed, phased, long-term planning and implementation process for sustainable socioeconomic-political development and (2) the achievement of a mutually agreed strategic geopolitical end state. Implementing this extraordinary set of challenges is not easy, quick, or cheap. It would, however, be far less demanding and costly in political, social, military, and monetary terms than allowing the problems of irresponsible governance and political instability to continue to fester and generate crises that work to the detriment of all concerned.[8]

VIGNETTE 1: PLANNING TO ACHIEVE STRATEGIC CLARITY: LESSONS THAT SHOULD HAVE BEEN LEARNED IN SOMALIA, 1992–1998

On December 3, 1992, the United Nations expanded its traditional role of peacekeeping operations to a more ambitious peace-enforcement intervention in an attempt to resolve the root causes and resultant violence in Somalia. In this first step by the international community to deal with the new post–Cold War phenomenon referred to as the "failed nation-state," participating members of the UN coalition were authorized to use "all necessary means" to carry out the Security Council mandates.

By the spring of 1993, what had begun as a mission to provide security for the delivery of humanitarian assistance was quickly evolving into one of nation building. However, the operation would undergo a major transformation in its structure and organization prior to taking on these new and substantially greater responsibilities. On May 4, 1993, the U.S.-led Unified Task Force (RESTORE HOPE) transferred control of the Somalia operation to the United Nations. This transformation was more than a change in leadership. It marked a planned turning point in the scope of the mission.

At transition, the new mandate of the Security Council Resolution 814 went into effect. That mission was to provide a secure environment not only for humanitarian relief efforts but also to achieve national reconciliation and a durable peace. That would require the establishment of a transnational government, as well as advance the rehabilitation of the economy. The significant additional tasks included the disarmament of the Somali militias and the return of hundreds of thousands of refugees to their homeland. These objectives implied a distinctly different end state from that given to the Unified Task Force, with very different implications for the military force committed to Somalia.[9]

Findings

By its very nature, the UNOSOM II mission would place the UN forces in direct opposition to one or more belligerent and effective clans that had been at war with each other for nearly two years. In particular, the UN forces would clash with those of Mohamed Farrah Hassan Aidid. He was a prominent clan leader who had his own political agenda regarding Somalia's future. He and his forces would act as a hegemonic nation-state and establish himself as the head of a new central government in the country. Within a week following the transition of the U.S. mission to the United Nations, Aidid's militia skirmished with the UN forces near the city of Kismayo. Three weeks later, his militia initiated a deliberate ambush on the UN forces in the capital city, Mogadishu. That resulted in the deaths of over 30 peacekeepers. This attack embroiled the United States in a protracted conflict that would ultimately end with the withdrawal of UNOSOM II from Somalia without accomplishing the UN-mandated mission. That mission was to end violence and factionalism and create the conditions necessary for political-economic-social development and sustainable peace. Essentially, that would mean going to war against Somalia.[10]

Response

If a condition for achieving unity of effort is agreement on and planning for achievement of a given strategic political objective, then UNOSOM II was in trouble from the beginning. Although this operation had a clearer mandate than its predecessor, the U.S.-led operation RESTORE HOPE, it was plagued by the fact that the administration of U.S. president Bill Clinton did not know exactly what it had signed on to. That was also the situation with the other participants. As the implications of the lack of a clear understanding of the mandate sank in, other players began to deny that they were indeed party to the agreement. The impact of this issue would only increase as time passed.

Lack of agreement on the meaning of the mandate was compounded by the command relationships that structured UNOSOM II. The UN operations usually employed a force under a single force commander appointed by the secretary general with the approval of the Security Council. The force commander reports either to the special representative of the secretary general or directly to the secretary general. While this is the norm, if a special representative is appointed, the force commander typically has a high degree of autonomy. The first deviation from the norm in terms of UNOSOM II was in the relationship between the special representative and the force commander. At the United States' insistence, the special representative was the former deputy national security adviser to the president of the United States, Admiral Jonathan Howe. The force commander was Lieutenant General Cevik Bir of Turkey. The deputy force commander was the U.S. major general Thomas Montgomery. He acted as commander of the U.S. forces in Somalia. This arrangement made for a particularly strong leadership role for Admiral Howe, essentially froze out Lieutenant General Bir, and made the command relationship an American operation in everything but name.[11]

Outcome

This command relationship and the UNOSOM II command and control structure proved ineffective. It did not help much that the Quick Reaction Force, located in Somalia, was under the operational control of the U.S. Central Command located in Florida. At the same time, some national contingents simply would not serve under the operational control of other contingent commanders. Instead, they would work "in coordination with" or "in cooperation with" other contingent forces. Not surprisingly, these command relationships proved ineffective.[12] Consequently, when the mandate given by Resolution 814 expanded to include the capture of Aidid (Resolution 837), several national force providers indicated that they had not agreed to use their forces for that purpose. This was demonstrated by Italy, which had maintained—and continued to maintain—a unilateral, direct dialogue with the leaders of Aidid's militia.

In short, UNOSOM II failed to achieve unity of effort as a result of the following three critical factors: (1) whatever agreement on the end-state objective that may have existed early on broke down following the passage of the UN Resolution 837, (2) the command and control arrangements were flawed, and (3) UNOSOM II had neither the military nor civilian capability to develop the conditions that would lead to the implementation of a coordinated plan for an effective nation-building. As a result, the entire confused process reverted to guerrilla warfare between Aidid's militia and the UNOSOM II forces.[13]

Implications and Conclusions

Somalia may be considered the first post–Cold War peace enforcement operation conducted by the international community. An examination of the case yields an analysis of a doomed operation. The failure to appropriately address the variables making up the unity of effort dimension of contemporary conflict guaranteed that there would be no chance of success. After a promising start by the Unified Task Force, unity of effort foundered on the shoals of a flawed command and control structure, lack of coordination among the parties making up UNOSOM II, and a profound lack of agreement regarding the objectives of that UN mission. The lack of unity of effort both influenced and reflected the ebbs and flows of the perceived legitimacy of the operation. While operation RESTORE HOPE had a high degree of legitimacy early on—owing in part to the agreement among all the UN and Somalian parties on the objective of humanitarian relief—UNOSOM II rapidly lost its legitimacy, as consent was withdrawn by one or another national contingent or one or another Somali militia.

The loss of consensus among the members of the UN coalition was soon reflected in the tacit and overt support given to Aidid by Italy, various Somali clans, and shadowy "Arab" factions. This, in turn, further weakened the strength of the UNOSOM II coalition. The changing degree of support for the operation was also reflected in the military actions of the peace force, as the various national and factional components of UNOSOM II sent negative signals regarding the effectiveness and focus of the UN effort. Thus, the inverse relationship between the increasing strength of Aidid's militia and the decreasing effectiveness of the several UNOSOM force contingents reflected the quality and quantity of the internal and external support Aidid was receiving. It also underscored the relative weakening of the UN force.

The inability of the several components of UNOSOM II to clearly identify the actions and means required to end the conflict greatly contributed to the failure of the operation. When the special representative to the secretary general of the United Nations and the force commander finally did identify the necessary actions and resources for their task, they could not get the other components to deliver what was needed in a timely fashion. What was finally accomplished was both too little and too late.[14]

Finally, the U.S.–UN organizational disarray was probably enough to guarantee defeat and withdrawal from Somalia. There was another problem, however. The fact that the United States and the United Nations were fighting an irrelevant war did not help achieve any level of strategic clarity. The U.S. and UN forces had all the best arms and equipment that money could buy. The Somalian militias were technologically backward. The U.S. and UN forces killed any number of militia personnel—not to mention innocent bystanders. The United States thought it was fighting a traditional war of attrition against a secondary military force made up of "skinnies" and "sommies." Yet, ultimately, the U.S. and UN forces acknowledged defeat and withdrew while the Somali militias emerged out of the population and took control of the country.[15]

KEY POINTS AND LESSONS

Key Points

- Personal and collective protection of a polity requires the military and police capability to provide an acceptable level of internal and external safety, the economic capacity to generate safety and socioeconomic development, and the political rectitude to develop the governance to which a given polity can relate and support.
- The keys that provide the means to go beyond simple protection to socioeconomic-political development are national development, end-state planning, and strategic clarity.
- End-state planning depends on an organizational management structure and the personnel with cognitive ability to respond to the dynamic political, economic, social, and military variables at work in the security-peace paradigm.
- Strategic clarity is the product of a complete unity of effort directed at the achievement of a mutually agreed upon geopolitical objective.
- Implementing these concepts is not easy, quick, or cheap. That will, however, be far less demanding and costly in political, economic, social, military, and monetary terms than allowing instability to fester and generate the murderous alternatives that work to the detriment of all concerned.

Lessons

The unity of effort/strategic clarity dimension of an unconventional—or conventional—war involves overcoming parochial bureaucratic interests, fighting "turf battles," and ensuring that all governmental and international organizational efforts are focused on the ultimate common goal—that is, survival. In these terms, a government must have the necessary organization to coordinate and implement an effective unity of political-diplomatic, socioeconomic, psychological-moral, and security-stability efforts against those who would destroy it. A government must also have the ability to accomplish these tasks in a manner acceptable to the people. Otherwise, as noted again, authority is fragmented and ineffective in resolving the myriad problems endemic to an irregular asymmetric assault on the state. The result would be state failure and the horrific aftermath of state failure. Somalia, 1992–1993, is a case in point.

Aidid and his allied militias had fought an unconventional asymmetric war that centered on a strong effort to convince the Somali people that the outside imposition of a new political-economic-social order was wrong, inappropriate, and not legitimate. Thus, Aidid won the "legitimacy war"—and the other wars within the general war as well.[16]

VIGNETTE 2: THE BRITISH AND AMERICAN EXPERIENCE IN BOSNIA, 1992–1998

Introduction and Context

When Marshall Josip Broz Tito died in 1980, the Yugoslavia that he created at the end of World War II had a real existence. The various peoples of the country were relatively united, and the six republics and two autonomous regions that made up the state were relatively prosperous. This was the result of Tito's authoritarian hand and his personal charisma. By 1989, this fragmented country began to experience a succession of five wars that lasted through the spring of 1999. Between 1991 and 1999, hundreds of thousands of Bosnian, Croats, Serbs, and Albanians were killed, raped, and/or tortured by one or another opposing faction. Millions were forced out of their homes and into internal or external exile. "Ethnic cleansing"—a new term for a very old practice—was utilized by all parties to the overall conflict. This was the general state of affairs in the former Yugoslavia in the early 1990s when the international community finally decided to try to do something (for something's sake).[17]

As noted often and elsewhere, the key to the implementation of a viable political-military stability strategy is end-state planning. This depends on a clear strategic vision of an agreed upon geopolitical objective, a close civil-military effort to achieve that objective, and the synchronization of those multidimensional efforts to attain the maximum power from that critical force multiplier. Decision makers, policy makers, opinion makers, planners, and implementers must also be concerned with the long-term effects of their efforts. And, they should never lose sight of the bigger picture. In these terms, it is useful to look into the British and American experience in the former Yugoslavia in the 1990s. These experiences provide good empirical examples of what can happen when end-state planning is ignored and what does happen when "ad hocery" is operative.

The British Experience: Findings, Response, and Outcome

The general officer who took command of the UN Protection Force (UNPROFOR) in Bosnia in 1995 was British general Rupert Smith. He was very direct. He states:

The starting point to understanding all operations in the Balkans in the 1990s, including the NATO bombings in 1995 and 1999, was that they were without strategies. At best, events were coordinated at theater level, but on the whole, especially with regard to the international interventions, they were reflexive—or functionalist, to use a term coined to understand the workings of the German Third Reich in World War II. Each event was a function of the one preceding it, rather than part of a plan, and whilst theoretically underpinned by the UN Security Council resolutions which laid out mandates, on the whole the forces deployed and employed, whether UN or NATO, were used in response to events on the ground rather than with a view to attaining a strategic objective. In fact, whatever political purposes the forces deployed into the Balkans served, they were not supporting goals directly related to a resolution of the conflict or confrontation in question. And, this was apparent from the start.[18]

The international rhetoric regarding the downward spiral of events and the international deployment within it was always strong and determined, but this translated into very little other than reinforced camps of international troops attempting to defend the delivery of humanitarian aid, and often themselves. There was no strategic direction, there was no strategic military goal to achieve, there was no military campaign, there was no theater-level military objectives: all acts were tactical. UNPROFOR opened up routes, secured and ran the Sarajevo airport and guarded convoys of aid. Yet over the years, and always in response to the events on the ground between the sides, more and more troops were sent in. By the time I assumed command in 1995, there were some 20,000 (the original deployment in 1992 was 5,000), all bound to their respective national headquarters and all prohibited from using force except in self-defense by the UN mandate and the ROE (Rules of Engagement).[19]

The events leading to the establishment of the "safe areas" in 1993 give a good example of the weakness of this arrangement. During 1992 the Bosniacs in the east of the country had maintained control of substantial areas of territory centered on the towns of Srebrenica and Gorazde and the village of Zepa. The humanitarian situation inside the areas was bad, a fact that that was used as part of the political play of the warring factions. As a UNHCR (UN High Commissioner for Refugees) explained ... "The Muslim pockets were used by the [Bosniac] Sarajevo government in November (1992) as pressure points on the international community for firmer action. The longer that aid convoys were unable to reach them, the greater the pressure on the mandate. When convoys did succeed, calls for firmer action were unwarranted. Two weeks after the first successful delivery Muslims [Bosniacs] launched an offensive towards Bratunac [a Serb-held town just outside the besieged Srebrenica]. Thus, the integrity of UNHCR and UNPROFOR was undermined, further convoys were impossible, and the pressure for firmer action resumed."[20]

This explanation, as indeed the situation reflects, shows how the UNHCR and UNPROFOR became caught in the first of what I came to call the hostage or shield situation that marked the story of UNPROFOR: they had no good choices. Lacking any form of strategic or theatre direction, nobody appears to have noticed the danger in which UNPROFOR stood. ... At the same time there was growing pressure to act on behalf of the refugees, as a direct result of the harrowing pictures on the TV screens. In light of these imperatives, and in retrospect, it seems to me that the most coherent imperative was the need to be seen to be doing something—"Something must be done" was a catchphrase of the times, and used exhaustively by politicians, diplomats and media as much as by the UN. It was this approach that blotted out a considered debate on the true dilemma facing the UN, which was caught between the sides in a hostage and shield situation, and the need to analyze why UNPROFOR was consistently failing to achieve its stated purpose.[21]

If "something must be done" became the main approach to the Balkan crisis, it was further complicated by the "something" being the desire to use air power which emanated from the U.S. Washington was increasingly involved in the debate as to what to do about the Balkans, not least due to a powerful lobby by the Bosniacs and the Croats. The U.S. stance was clear: it did not want to be involved on the ground, and equally saw no need to be neutral with regard to the sides. The TV pictures of Bosnian Serb aircraft attacking refugee columns was enough to have an NFZ (No Fly Zone) declared over Bosnia by the UN in October 1992, and in April 1993, led by the U.S., NATO undertook to police the zone aerially and mounted Operation Deny Flight. ... However, this initiative created a command and control dilemma. If a student at any military staff college in the world produced a plan that had forces operating in the same space answering to two different chains of command he might, if he was lucky, to be told to try again—but more probably he would have his cards marked "fail." Having a NATO NFZ over and within a UN operation created this very situation. The NATO planners therefore had to find a way to link the two command chains so that UN-authorized flights were not attacked, and when NATO attacks were made UN units were alerted to the possibility of retaliatory attacks. NATO's solution came to be called the "dual key" procedures, within which both the senior NATO and UNPROFOR commanders in the region had to approve a NATO operation. In the summer of 1995, I became the commander who turned the UNPROFOR key.[22]

These events in the spring of 1995 held within them all the components of UNPROFOR's involvement in the sorry tale of the subsequent two and a half years. ... [C]ommander after commander stood between the parties to the war, attempting to discharge his orders to support the delivery of aid, yet finding himself in one variation or another in the position of an inevitable hostage and shield situation. ... At base the nations, and therefore the international organizations, were not willing to act forcefully with the measures they had put in place, nor to create the overarching diplomatic and political structures which would have given them substance.[23]

The American Experience: Implications and Conclusions

The American general officer who was given command of the U.S. and NATO forces in Bosnia in the mid-1990s was Lieutenant General William G. Carter III. Like General Smith, he was quite candid to the point and told a similar story. Instead of recounting much of General Smith's narrative, however, let us consider the guidance Lieutenant General Carter received from the U.S. secretary of defense prior to taking his assignment in the Balkans. That guidance explains quite a lot.

I went to dinner with [the Secretary of Defense]. I was commander of the 1st Armored Division at the time, but I had been told in 1993 that I was going to take command in Sarajevo. I asked [the Secretary] "What is it that you want me to do?" I was kind of surprised in a way and not surprised in another way that he had no answer to that. He had really not thought through what was the end-state or whatever. So, I said, "OK, here is what I can offer you. If you will give me some degree of latitude as to just how ruthless I can be, I can go in and do a good replication of Marshall Tito. I can go in and I can clamp down that country and I can stop the bloodshed. I can stop the fighting. I can disarm the factions." I said that "the downside of this is that I am going to have to stay forever, because just like Marshall Tito, when I leave all the latent hatred will still be there and it will go back to some kind of conflict. So, I can stabilize it, if that is what you want me to do. So, what is it you want me to do?" Then, [the Secretary] said, "What we want you to do," and he was being very pragmatic, "is get it the hell off CNN."[24]

With that guidance, it should come as no surprise that the U.S. military coordination during the assessment and plan development phases of operations in the former Yugoslavia did not involve the key U.S. governmental organizations, international organizations, coalition partners, or nongovernmental organizations. Later, planning and implementing procedures broke down in the face of competing national interests and institutional agendas, as well as segregated planning and implementing processes. Moreover, in the absence of a single overarching political-military campaign plan, ad hoc reaction to changing conditions and "mission creep" became the norm. As a result, there was no strategic clarity (i.e., unity of effort) and very limited effectiveness.

KEY POINTS AND LESSONS

Key Points

Even though every conflict situation differs in time, place, and circumstance, none is truly unique. Certain analytical commonalities can be seen. For example:

- By definition, independent uncoordinated "stove pipe" planning and implementation processes prevent unity of effort.
- They also sow confusion, require counterproductive "quick fixes" that contribute to the duplication and triplication of effort, and add significantly to the political, monetary, and personnel costs of any given civil-military operation.

- Thus, the outcome of a conflict such as that in the former Yugoslavia is not determined primarily by the skillful manipulation of violence on the battlefield.
- Rather, control of the situation and its resolution is determined by the qualitative leader judgments and the synergistic processes established before, during, and after a conflict is politically recognized to have begun.

Lessons

The aforementioned key points relate to the essential components of strategic clarity and unity of effort. And, as difficult as it may be to achieve, strategic clarity is an essential commonality for achieving success in modern conflict and creating a sustainable foundation for peace. Finally, the venerable general Carl von Clausewitz warned us many years ago that "War plans cover every aspect of conflict and weave them into a single operation that must have a single, ultimate objective in which all particular aims are reconciled. No one starts a war (i.e., conflict)—or rather, no one in his right senses ought to do so—without first being clear in his mind what he intends to achieve, and how he is going to achieve it."[25]

CHAPTER 4

Stability and Development: Lessons from Argentina (1960–Present) and Mexico (1999–Present) —Attacking the State from Within

In the past, developed countries generally provided short-term economic and financial aid to developing countries under the assumption that personal and collective security and political-economic-social development would automatically follow. That has not happened. Rather, experience teaches that long-term, multilevel, and multilateral capability-building measures are the bases through which competent and honest political leadership can effectively provide individual and collective well-being. It is under these conditions that a responsible governing regime can begin to develop a durable peace and prosperity. On the other side of that proverbial coin, an adversary can attack those same measures to destabilize and perhaps to destroy a given socioeconomic-political system. This objective can be accomplished indirectly and subtly over a long period of time and can be considerably less violent than a conventional insurgency war. In this context, we review the following: (1) threats to stability and security, (2) the relationship of stability and development, (3) some "new" security realities, and (4) the notion of what can be done. Then to illustrate this issue, we provide two examples of internal nonstate actors attacking the state from within.

The first almost bloodless example is that of the Argentine *Piquetero* organization. Its stated intention has been to take down the government and create a revolutionary "new" (Peronist) Argentina. The second model could not be more different. It is direct and anything but subtle. It is unconscionably violent, and the strategic geopolitical objective is to "control"—not take down—a "democratically elected" government for short-term commercial self-serving purposes—that is, the case of the Mexican *Zetas*.

THREATS TO STABILITY AND SECURITY

The moral right of a regime to govern focuses on the concept of a "social contract." The social contract as articulated by the venerable Jean-Jacques Rousseau in traditional political theory is maintained through the continuing consent of the governed. It is also maintained through the continuing acceptance and support provided by a country's social institutions. That consent and support is dependent on governments acting in a morally acceptable manner. Experience teaches us that Rousseau was right. Long-term, multilevel, and multilateral capability-building measures are the bases through which competent and responsible political leadership can effectively provide for the individual and collective well-being.[1] It is under these conditions—protected by the kind of stability discussed in Chapters 1, 2, and 3—that a responsible governing regime can begin to develop sustainable peace and well-being (i.e., security). This works two ways, however. The elements that generate national stability and well-being are the elements an adversary will seek to destroy in order to achieve his or her objectives of radical change and/or personal enrichment—and to leave the social contract in shreds.

In these terms, irregular and very unconventional actors playing in a national security arena generate the same strategic-level geopolitical threats to stability, development, and security as the actors playing in the global security arena. These irregular actors attack the same elements of the peace-security equation that legitimate governance tries to develop and enhance. These actors also understand that public opinion and political leadership are the hubs of all power on which everything depends (i.e., the center of gravity). At the same time, these actors also realize that their strategic geopolitical objective must be to co-opt, persuade, control, and/or otherwise coerce public opinion to accept one's will. The more skillfully this is done, the more freedom of movement and action the irregular actor enjoys. And, as a consequence, the irregular actor is more likely to achieve his or her desired strategic geopolitical end state.

At the operational and tactical levels, the objectives noted in Chapter 2, and again in this chapter, represent a quintuple threat to the authority, legitimacy, and stability of targeted societies and governments. Generally, these threats include the following: (1) undermining the ability of government to perform its legitimizing functions; (2) changing a government's foreign, defense, and other policies; (3) isolating religious or racial communities from the rest of the society and beginning to replace traditional state authority with alternative governance; (4) transforming socially isolated human terrain into self-governing "virtual states" within the host state; and (5) conducting low-cost actions calculated to maximize damage, minimize response, and display carefully staged media events that lead to the erosion of the legitimacy and stability of a targeted state's political-economic-social system. At the same time, there is the resultant humanitarian disaster that would be the sum and substance of the aftermath of contemporary conflict and state failure.[2]

THE RELATIONSHIP OF STABILITY AND DEVELOPMENT

The international security dialogue focuses on development and national reconstruction as a means to deal with the threat problem. That requirement equates to a long-term holistic capability-building effort. The fulfillment of that kind of imperative provides the capacity for the nation-state to generate the socioeconomic-political strength necessary to provide internal order and progress (i.e., stability). That imperative consists of three long-term strategic-level programs that are necessary to free and protect a people from lawlessness and violence—as well as the aftermath of violence. As stated in Chapter 1, they are to develop the following: (1) the police-military capability to provide an acceptable level of individual and collective security/stability, (2) the socioeconomic-political ability to generate national development and reconstruction, and (3) the political capability to develop a type of governance to which a people can relate and support. These programs constitute the basis for a realistic and pragmatic approach focused on the circular relationship of legitimate governance to stability, the relationship of stability to development, the relationship of development to political competence, and the relationship of political competence back to security and stability. The intent is to build viable institutions that respond to the needs of a society and strengthen governance. That is, one more time, $S = (M + E \times PC)$.[3]

Additionally, at least four of the five operational-level variables must be brought into play in order to generate the responsible political competence that can and will generate, manage, coordinate, and sustain stability and national development. These supporting variables would include the following: (1) reduce perceived and real corruption, (2) foster well-being and political consent, (3) hold free, fair, and frequent elections, (4) establish and maintain popularly accepted peaceful societal conflict-resolution processes, and (5) foster regime acceptance by major social institutions. With all these capability-building blocks in place within the basic E component of the equation, a civil society and sustainable peace become genuine possibilities.[4] On the other hand, without basic stability, logic and the math tell us that there will be little or no development.

REVIEWING SOME "NEW" SECURITY REALITIES

The traditional distinctions between crime, terrorism, subversion, insurgency, popular militia, mercenary and gang activity, and warfare are blurred. Underlying these ambiguities is the fact that most of these activities tend to be intrastate affairs (i.e., not issues between sovereign nation-states) that international law and convention are only beginning to address. None of this is new. As noted earlier and will be repeated again and again, many civilian and military leaders do not want to deal with these issues. Like it or not, however, these realities must be acknowledged and dealt with sooner or later.

First, contemporary conflict, more often than not, is an internal problem that sets one segment of society against another. Although war can be defined in various ways, war is most authoritatively defined as the coercion of one party by another.[5]

Second, overwhelming empirical evidence illustrates that the essence of any given contemporary threat situation relies heavily on perceived popular political-economic-social grievances as the primary means through which a vulnerable state or nonstate actor is or is not successfully attacked. Again, we note with Carl von Clausewitz that public opinion and political leadership are the hubs of all power on which everything depends (i.e., the center of gravity)[6]—that is, public opinion is the primary center of gravity in contemporary conflict and the "ends" of a modern ends, ways, and means strategy must be to co-opt, persuade, control, and/or compel an adversary's public opinion to accept one's will. In that connection, empirical evidence and logic dictate that legitimate governance is the central strategic problem in the contemporary global security environment. As a result, we also find that there are other ways besides military to influence and control public opinion and political leadership. Again, the key to influencing popular perceptions is to demonstrate that legitimate governmental authority does or does not in fact serve public political-economic-social needs and is or is not applied in a morally correct manner.[7]

Third, in this "new" security environment, war is no longer the only instrument of state policy but also of personal belief, feeling, whim, or grudge. War is no longer the only instrument exercised by the state but also by small organized groups (e.g., individual nonstate players). Coercive war can take a hundred different forms and is no longer so monetarily expensive that only wealthy nation-states can afford to become involved. War is no longer an exclusive military undertaking that is regulated arbitrarily by the major world powers. War, kinetic or nonkinetic, declared or undeclared, remains, however, an act of coercion to compel an adversary to do one's will. As a consequence, and at base, the enemy is now the political actor who plans and implements the multidimensional kinds of indirect and direct, nonmilitary and military, and nonlethal and lethal, internal and external activities that threaten a given society's general political-economic-social well-being and exploit the root causes of instability. The primary and specific effort that ultimately breaks up and defeats an adversary's political-economic-social system and compels radical change is a legitimizing multidimensional erosion of people's morale and political will. And, once again we note that the better a protagonist is at conducting this persuasive-coercive effort, the more effective that protagonist will be relative to the opposition. Accordingly, as Clausewitz taught, the contemporary primary center of gravity changes from a familiar military concept to an ambiguous and uncomfortable legitimacy, leadership, and public opinion paradigm that includes an acceptable level of political-economic-social well-being.[8]

Fourth, in striving to establish or counter these destabilizing conditions, irregular belligerent nonstate and rogue-state actors now seek to establish conditions that drain and exhaust their opponents. Power, as a result, is no longer simply combat firepower directed at an enemy soldier or industrial complex. Power is a multilevel—a combined political, psychological, moral, informational, economic, social, military, police, and civil-bureaucratic—activity that can be brought to bear appropriately on the causes as well as the perpetrators of violence. The desired result may be achieved by those individuals familiar with Sun Tzu's "indirect approach" and Professor Joseph Nye's "smart power" approach to contemporary security—that is, brain power that includes an understanding of diverse cultures, an appreciation of the power of dreams, and a mental flexibility that goes well beyond traditional forms of "muddling through."[9]

Fifth, the principle instruments of power in this situation would include—but not be limited to—such things as intelligence operations, public diplomacy at home and abroad, and economic and financial measures. Additionally, information and propaganda operations and cultural and cyber manipulation measures have proven to be very effective in influencing and/or controlling public opinion and decision-making leadership. Foreign alliances, partnerships, and traditional diplomacy are also very useful. It must be remembered that Germany's former chancellor, Helmut Kohl, breached the legendary Berlin Wall with the powerful Deutsche Mark—not aircraft, artillery, armor, or infantry. As a consequence, Qiao Liang and Wang Xiangsui stress that national and international security is no longer an exclusive "imperial garden" where professional soldiers alone can mingle. Nonprofessional warriors such as cyber warriors, hackers, financiers, media experts, software engineers, biologists, and criminals are taking on larger and larger roles every day in the national and global security arenas.[10]

Sixth, many political, military, and opinion leaders involved in the global security arena have been struggling with these "new" aspects of security-peace phenomenon for years. They have been slow to understand how governments might ultimately control—or succumb to—the coercive terroristic threats inherent in contemporary unrestricted intranational and international conflict. To help achieve this understanding, however, leaders and the informed public must know something of who and what they might be dealing with. One can take an important step toward understanding the unconventional criminal-insurgent-terrorist wars in our midst by examining two very different but similar cases in point. But, first, let us take a quick look at the question or statement of what might be done in order to become more effective in the contemporary global security arena.

WHAT IS TO BE DONE

This is not a question; it is a statement. In the long term, the people and government of a fragile, failing, or failed state must save themselves from themselves. In the short term, however, a vulnerable people or government will likely require outside help. The learned professor Amitai Etzioni cautions us that intervening powers must also apply the principle of responsible sovereignty with the understanding that they cannot bring about liberal democratic states overnight. Experience should also remind us that social engineering projects are best undertaken by carefully guided internal actors. Moreover, objectives need to be tempered to match both local and international political-economic constraints. Outsiders and domestic leaders must rely on local customs, politics, and practices to establish new institutions that can move over the long term toward international norms of transparent, accountable, and responsible governance.[11]

At the same time, the earliest phases of an intervention must include a transition strategy, not an exit policy. Transition requires clearly delineated stabilizing, socioeconomic, and political development milestones. With this under control, local and international authorities can focus on the broader long-term challenges of reconstruction, political reconciliation, socioeconomic development, professionalization and modernization of the state bureaucracy, and the development of political competence on a foundation of moral legitimacy. Otherwise, declaring victory, going home, and leaving a country without consistent and vigilant guidance tend to result in a sectarian or partisan autocracy leading a state into failure and/or civil war—or another foreign intervention. This kind of scenario has also been known to precipitate regimes that protect themselves rather than the people of the country.

As noted elsewhere, all this does not mean that the United States must be involved all over the world all the time. It does mean, however, that the United States must rethink and renew its concept of security, in much the same way that Ambassador George F. Kennan's Containment

Theory of Engagement with the Soviet Union was conceived in 1947. Philosophical underpinnings must be devised for a new policy to deal with more diverse threats—from unpredictable directions and by more diverse state and nonstate actors.[12] Clearly, the United States and its allies have the responsibility to understand and implement the strategies that bring prosperity and peace to the rest of the world—before even more people become emigrants, refugees, or pensioners of the West. Yet, an enforced peace can provide only the beginning environment from which to start political reconciliation, economic reconstruction, and moral legitimization processes. Counselor Joseph N. McBride would suggest that the best that might be expected is to establish a level of security that results in the sustainable development of ethical and professional political competence. [13]

VIGNETTE 1: THE ARGENTINE *PIQUETEROS*

Introduction and Context

The Argentine *Piquetero* "rent-a-mobs"—or agents for radical political change, depending on how you look at them—have demonstrated how a state-supported set of pseudo-militias (i.e., agitation and propaganda— "agitprop"—groups) can (1) remain connected with their state sponsors through a system of networks and an overarching political agenda; (2) conduct high-damage, low-cost actions calculated for measured public intimidation and effective political damage to the state; (3) provide no official armed force to attack, no physical territory to take and hold; and (4) appear and disappear within a population in an instant.

Professor Guillermo Gini of the *Universidad Católica de Argentina* tells us that the "seeds of the *Piquetero* movement were sown in the 1960s by Catholic priests involved in the Liberation Theology Movement. At that time, these very small and loosely organized groups were concerned with the problems of equitable income, and land and property distribution. Main efforts centered on helping squatters gain legal title to occupied properties, advocating extensive public works projects for job creation, and campaigning for the social values of Liberation Theology."[14] Later in the 1970s, at the time of Argentina's "Dirty War," most of the relatively inconsequential organizations that would come to be known as "*Piqueteros*" were assimilated into the Peronist *Montonero* insurgent organization. A few went into the communist People's Liberation Army (i.e., EPL). During that violent and polarized intrastate conflict, strong Peronist identities were forged. Various Argentine labor unions and parts of the government bureaucracy are still dominated by individuals whose formative political life was informed by Peronist political tutelage.

Findings

During the 1980s and through the early 2000s, unemployed workers organized into militant neighborhood unions (i.e., groups or gangs). Then, after regaining access to public office in 1983, Peronist politicians began to use state resources to secure alliances with neighborhood political brokers (i.e., *punteros*) and develop patronage-based support networks (i.e., *agrupaciones*) to strengthen their control on both party and government. The availability of public money and more than enough unemployed workers generated some rapid and far-reaching effects: (1) *puntero* leaders reportedly flocked to the *agrupaciones* and converted themselves and their lieutenants into government employees; (2) the Peronists built a powerful political machine, and clientelist networks replaced *agrupaciones* as "plausibly deniable" instruments of illicit party and government power; (3) in 1996, President Carlos Menem reorganized the basis of the patronage-client networks, that is, under *Plan Trabajar* (i.e., work plan for monthly subsidies to unemployed workers), subsidies were provided in exchange for some sort of service to the state; (4) since the *plans* come from the government and the government has the leverage to ask for something in return, *Piqueteros* have acted as government agents (i.e., mercenary gangs) for all kinds of populist "disruption" activities; and (5) unemployed *Piqueteros* have proved ready, willing, and able to organize diffuse actions that could possibly prove embarrassing to targeted government organizations—depending on the "rent-a-mob" requirements of the moment.

These "disruption" projects have ranged from general protest, marches, and riots to occupation of public buildings, factories, and businesses to blocking specific streets, roads, and highways. At the same time, *Piqueteros* have been used to participate in larger mass protests, mobilizing several thousand militants. As an important example, a combination of center and left-of-center groups and *Piqueteros* joined together in December 2001 to bring about the "popular impeachment" of two presidents of the Republic—Fernando de la Rua and Adolfo Rodriguez Saa—within a period of 10 days. Additionally, during the Nestor Kirchner administration, half the members of the Supreme Court were forced from office, with a little help from Kirchner's *Piquetero* friends.[15]

Outcome: Piquetero "Disruption," the Road to Dignity, and a New Argentina

The agitation-propaganda (i.e., agitprop) activities noted earlier are not considered to be a form of civil disobedience or simple collective resistance against grievances, insensitive or misguided governance, or any kind of insurrection. The operative word is "disruption." Behind the destabilizing populist actions that define "disruption," there is an explicit political agenda. Generally, *Piqueteros* have claimed that they do not want governmental power. They state that they are not interested in being included in a political system based on exploitation and repression of the people. For them the starting point for changing Argentina is the construction of something new from below. That aim would be to go beyond the struggle for equitable income distribution, jobs, and sociopolitical "inclusion." The ultimate *Piquetero* objective is to achieve "dignity." Dignity is defined as a political system that will orient the government and the economy toward the needs of the people. That objective requires the destruction of the current state system and the creation of a New Argentina.

Even though *Piqueteros* have shouted invective, carried heavy sticks, worn masks, painted their faces, broken windows, thrown rocks and other projectiles, and looked and acted very fierce, they have stayed just below the threshold of unacceptable violence. *Piqueteros* understand that they cannot directly attack the state and its security organizations. In his *Changing the World without Taking Power*, John Holloway outlines a strategy that might change Argentina. He argues that by indirectly assaulting the foundations of the state with soft counterpower, an organization controlled by direct democracy can slowly weaken the state, dissolve what is left of Argentine liberal democracy and the capitalist economy, and radically change the entire political-economic-social system. At that point, a new and better Peronist state and political-economic system can be created. *Piqueteros* call this antistate strategy "disruption." The disruptive soft power political agenda begins with the kinds of agitprop efforts that the *Piqueteros* have done best—that is, they have generated low-level violence and political-psychological efforts designed to break the bonds between a government and its people. These efforts are designed to slowly generate the "correlation of forces" that, in turn, enables dignity and a New Argentina. Paradoxically, the Argentine government has subsidized *Piqueteros* to maintain stability, and it also has paid these individuals to destabilize the system. These distortions operate on two negative levels—antiliberal democracy and antistate stability. Interestingly and importantly, the resultant New Argentina would look a lot like the revolutionary state advocated by Vladimir Ilyich Lenin.[16]

Conclusions: Where the Peronist and *Piquetero* Contradictions Lead

If empirical reality is any guide, then Holloway is only partly right. One can create the conditions that define a correlation of forces that can eventually lead to radical political change. Nevertheless, it is likely that one or another internal or external political actor will sooner or later want to take the level of power that can hurry that change. The two most likely contenders in Argentina are the well-organized Peronists and the more fractious *Piqueteros*. Argentine Peronists have found the *Piqueteros* to be useful in fomenting partisan actions. At the same time, *Piqueteros* have found government subsidies and mercenary destabilization tasks to be helpful and supportive in their personal needs and antiliberal and anti-system strategies. It would appear that either the government and its client *Piquetero* organizations are collaborating in the erosion of democracy and the state or there are those in government who expect to control the evolution of the correlation of forces for their own purposes. Of course, there may be *Piqueteros* who expect that their counterpower may eventually be capable of controlling and diminishing government power. It is probably impossible to determine how this distortion might work out. History continually teaches us, however, that the actor most likely to win any given conflict is the one that is best prepared cognitively and organizationally. In these terms, one might expect that the Peronists would be the winners if the Peronist-*Piquetero* partnership devolves into an internal conflict. But, in politics, things can change quickly. The one thing that looks to be certain in this situation is that the future of liberal democracy and sustained peace in Argentina is not bright.[17]

KEY POINTS AND LESSONS

Key Points

- The Argentine *Piqueteros* demonstrate how a state-supported set of "gangs" might fit into a holistic state or nonstate actor's effort to compel internal radical political-economic-social change.

- The *Piquetero* unemployed workers' movement has flourished in that political environment. In that environment, the government—or key individuals in it—provides resources that allow *Piquetero* existence. The intent is to subsidize unemployed workers to maintain political stability and also, paradoxically, to destabilize the system.

- These distortions work on two levels: antiliberal democracy and an antistate system. That dual-level process compels slow and deliberate movement toward radical political-economic-social change.

- As a result, the Argentine political system is not being attacked by any kind of external enemy or traditional insurgency. It is being attacked from within by those who use liberal-democratic freedoms, institutions, and money to further their radical ambitions to create a New Argentina.

Lessons

In *The Lessons of History*, one of Clausewitz's translators, Michael Howard, warns us that, in the past, these kinds of internal subversive measures have led to fascist solutions. He would have asked the question: "Is there any reason to suppose the Peronist officials working in the Argentine government and their *Piquetero* allies will do better?"[18]

VIGNETTE 2: THE MEXICAN ZETAS

Introduction

The Mexican Zetas represent our second model for taking internal control of human and physical terrain. This criminal organization does not pretend to change or reform an unjust order or redress perceived grievances. The stated intent is to achieve complete freedom of movement and action in order to maximize illicit commercial profits. As a consequence, they must destroy, neutralize, or control any other nonstate or state competitor that might stand in the way of achieving their self-enrichment objective. These violent politicized nonstate actors operate in accordance with a political logic that is (1) a continuation of politics by direct, irregular, and very violent means; (2) not a test of expertise in creating instability and fear but rather an exercise in illicit self-enrichment; (3) intended to compel control of physical and human terrain; and (4) inadvertently a force for coercing radical systemic change.

Context

Transnational criminal organizations (TCOs) such as the traditional drug cartels, *Mara Salvatrucha* 13 (i.e., MS-13) and *Mara Salvatrucha* 18 (i.e., MS-18), the mafia, enforcer gangs, vigilante organizations, and individual triggermen (*gatilleros*) are not the only nonstate actors in Mexico and the Western Hemisphere that exercise violence to radicalize the population, neutralize the state, and move decisively toward the achievement of self-enrichment dreams. There is a relatively new and dangerous nonstate pseudo-military criminal organization hard at work within these security environments—that is, the Mexican *Zetas*. What makes irregular nonstate actors, such as the *Zetas*, so effective is the absence of anyone for victims or potential victims to turn to for help. Weak and/or corrupt state security institutions, as in Mexico, are notoriously unhelpful and tend to be a part of the problem—not the solution. In such a vacuum, leaders of these quasi-state political entities promulgate their own rule of law, negotiate alliances, and conduct an irregular insurgency-type war against state and nonstate adversaries. Additionally, criminal quasi-states force victimized populations to adapt to an ambivalent and precarious existence that challenges traditional values and individual and collective security.[19]

Findings: *Zeta* Organization and Operations

The origins of the *Zeta* organization date back to 1999. The Gulf Drug Cartel recruited members of the Mexican Army's elite Airborne Special Forces Group (GAFE). The GAFE members who defected to the cartel called themselves *Los Zetas*. The intent of the cartel's recruitment effort was to provide effective protection from government forces and other cartels. The Gulf Cartel paid the *Zetas* salaries well beyond those paid by the army to make desertion worth their while. The idea proved to be a great success. Once the former soldiers were in place and functioning, their superior training, organization, equipment, experience, and discipline led them from simple protection missions to operations that were more challenging. *Zetas* began to collect Gulf Cartel debts, secure drug trafficking routes that once belonged to other cartels, discourage defections from other parts of the cartel organization, and track down and execute particularly troublesome rival cartel and other gang leaders all over Mexico and Central America. Subsequently, the *Zetas* expanded their activities to kidnapping, human trafficking, arms trafficking, money laundering, creating secure new trafficking routes to and from the United States and Europe, as well as developing exclusive access to cocaine sources in South America. All this has been accomplished by using terrorist tactics—and just plain murder and torture—often with grotesque savagery.

In February 2010, *Los Zetas* followed a pattern established and used by mercenary organizations for hundreds of years. They broke away from their employer and formed their own cartel. Subsequently, they have developed their own very effective flat organization, their own agenda and timetable, and their own protective mystique. These measures have allowed a relatively small force to accomplish the following objectives: (1) convince the people of a given area that the *Zeta* organization—not local politicians or local police, federal authorities, and other cartels—is the real power in that specific geographical terrain; (2) exert authority within its defined area of operations—even if not physically present at any given moment; and (3) fight both a larger force—police or military— and another political actor at the same time.

Over the long term, the *Zetas'* first priority is to operate a successful business enterprise, with more than adequate self-protection and self-promotion. This private criminal-military organization encourages diversification of activities, diffusion of risk, and the flexibility to make quick adjustments, correct mistakes, and exploit developing opportunities. The organization can deliberately expand or contract to adjust to specific requirements and to new allies or enemies—while increasing profits. And, of course, this organization maintains a coherent security mechanism for safeguarding operations at all levels and enforcing discipline throughout the structure. Consequently, over the past several years, the *Zetas* have decisively moved from protecting the Gulf Cartel to conducting an ambitious expansion policy of its own. That expansion has taken the *Zetas* into new territories and markets in Mexico, Central America, and elsewhere in the Western Hemisphere and into Africa, Europe, and Russia.[20]

Outcome: Where These "Bad Guys" Lead

After reviewing the basic facts of the brutal methods, the *Zetas* use to insinuate their power over people and institutions; one can see that these seemingly random and senseless criminal acts have specific political-psychological objectives. This organization does not appear to be intent on completely destroying the traditional Mexican state political-economic-social system and replacing that system with its own. Rather, and as noted earlier, the *Zetas* pursue a less radical option. It seeks to incrementally "capture" the state. To accomplish this aim, the leadership have determined that—at a minimum—they need to be able to freely travel, communicate, transfer funds, and move goods all around the globe. For this, they need to be within easy reach of functioning communication and banking centers. At the same time, the *Zetas* are not interested in replacing the government with its own. There is not a lot of excitement or profit in having to run the local waterworks or power plants. Thus, the *Zetas* do not find the completely failed state particularly useful. They would prefer to have Mexico as a weak but moderately functional international entity. Additionally, Mexican state weakness provides two very important advantages. First, that weakness provides the *Zetas* freedom to operate with almost complete impunity. Second, the international legal shell of traditional state sovereignty protects the *Zetas* from outside (i.e., the United States) intervention.

Conclusions

Importantly, it should be added that trafficking in illegal drugs, arms, precious metals, oil, timber, and human beings generates a hefty cash flow that enables a covert narco-government alliance. That cash flow generates liquidity for the state and profits for legal and illegal transnational organizations and institutions. Consequently, that liquidity becomes the main economic engine of organized crime and a major contributor to gross domestic product (GDP) for the state. Control, then, works as a system of private arrangements between government, plutocratic businesses, and TCOs. The absence of transparency and accountability to the public defines a cruel, cynical, violent, unjust, and undemocratic criminal bazaar that can most charitably be called a pseudo-democracy.[21]

KEY POINTS AND LESSONS

Key Points

- A new and dangerous dynamic has been introduced into the global security environment. That new dynamic involves the migration of power from the traditional state and nonstate adversaries to irregular criminal nonstate actors such as the *Zetas*.

- These irregular quasi-state actors promulgate their own rule of law, negotiate alliances with traditional nation-state and nonstate actor, and conduct armed conflict against various state and nonstate competitors. In this case, component parts of the TCO and *Zeta* phenomena are at war with each other and with the Mexican government.

- Commercial enrichment is the primary objective of the *Zetas* (and other TCOs). There is no great desire to destroy the traditional Mexican political-economic-social system. Rather, the *Zetas* pursue a less radical option. They seek to incrementally "capture" the state.

- Mexican state weakness provides two very important advantages. First, it provides TCOs the freedom to operate with impunity. Second, the shell of traditional Westphalian state sovereignty protects the *Zetas* from outside (i.e., the United States) intervention.

- The resultant erosion of democracy and the state takes the internal security and stability situation in Mexico well beyond a simple law enforcement problem. It is a socioeconomic-political problem and also a national security issue with serious implications beyond Mexican borders.

Lessons: A Cautionary Tale

State failure is an evolutionary process, not an outcome. This process can be exacerbated by nonstate and state actors that want to depose a targeted government or exercise illicit control over a given country or parts of it. And, over time, a targeted government and its institutions become progressively less capable of performing its legitimizing tasks of governance—including exercising fundamental personal and collective security and well-being functions.

Under these conditions, democracy erodes, and as a consequence, crediting elections of governments as "democratic" becomes problematic. At the same time, when corrupt civilian and military politicians and bureaucrats favor themselves, their friends, and relatives rather than the public they are supposed to serve, democracy decays. When unscrupulous actors compete violently to control government by murdering, kidnapping, intimidating, and/or corrupting political candidates and office holders before and after elections, democracy becomes a joke. When the state is guilty of failure to deal effectively with thuggish and brutal repression of basic human rights, democracy becomes a farce and the social contract is broken. In these situations, the state is not in control of its national territory or the people in it. Accordingly, the state forfeits its de facto and de jure sovereignty, and the best-organized, best-disciplined, and best-armed adversary takes control. That control leads directly to the coerced imposition of a radical socioeconomic-political restructuring of the state, and an accompanying radical change in the authoritative allocation of values for the society. That change, of course, would be in accordance with the good, bad, or nonexistent values of the adversary. This is the reality of where it is that the "bad guys" lead.[22]

CHAPTER 5

Development and Governance: Lessons from Vietnam (1959–1975) and Algeria (1954–1962) — Recreating the Conditions That Lead to the Moral Right to Take Control of Government

As noted in the previous discussion of the social contract, unless and until a population perceives that its government deals with the issues of security, well-being, and development fairly and effectively, the potential for internal—and possibly external—forces to destabilize and subvert a regime is considerable. Regimes that ignore these lessons often find themselves in a "crisis of governance"—that is, facing social violence, criminal anarchy, terrorism, and the potential for internal insurgency and/or foreign intervention.

The most cogent issues emerging out of this holistic legitimacy war concept take us a little deeper into the fundamental building blocks that take us to the following: (1) the stabilization and regeneration of the economy, (2) the cultivation of a civil society, and (3) the kind of political development that leads to responsible governance and a sustainable peace. These are the ways and means by which a state might defeat—or succumb to—a given crisis of governance. These are also the ways and means by which a state can gain the allegiance of the people and make its adversaries irrelevant—or not. A good example from which to learn how a government and its foreign allies might defeat or succumb to a given crisis of governance is that of Vietnam, 1959–1975. General Vo Nguyen Giap explains how it was that the militarily weaker North Vietnamese were able to overcome and prevail over the militarily stronger United States and South Vietnamese adversary in the following terms: "The Vietnamese people's war of liberation was victorious because it was a just war . . . in the legitimate interests of the people." He went on to say, "If the Vietnamese war of liberation ended in glorious victory, it was because we did not fight alone. We fought with the support of the progressive peoples the world over."[1]

The accompanying vignette, Public Opinion and Political Leadership, Vietnam, 1959–1975, elaborates on the fundamental disconnect between the U.S. policy and the reality of contemporary conflict. The United States thought it was fighting a traditional war of attrition against a secondary military force wearing funny black pajamas. Thus, the Americans fought to increase enemy "body count." The Vietcong and their external allies focused their attention on a full-scale media-propaganda-diplomatic war directed at local and world public opinion. They fought to establish the conditions that would lead to the political-moral right to take control of the entire Vietnamese state and secure full independence. The end result was that the United States and its South Vietnamese allies won all the battles. The North Vietnamese and its Vietcong allies won the war.[2] Additionally, we provide another example of a similar but different approach to the kind of political-psychological development that leads to responsible governance and a sustainable peace—that is, the political-psychological decolonization lessons from Algeria, 1954–1962.

STABILIZATION AND REGENERATION OF THE ECONOMY

Legitimate (responsible) governance is more than de facto or de jure legitimacy. *Legitimate governance* is defined as governance that derives its just powers from the governed. The assumption is that this kind of governance can and will generate a viable political competence that can and will manage, coordinate, and sustain political-economic-social development. That, in turn, enables the individual and collective well-being that defines stability. That stability is the foundation upon which security and a sustainable peace are built.[3]

The first phase of generating responsible legitimacy and governance is to gain control of a given polity. The second phase is stabilization. Stabilization is critical and requires taking immediate action to enforce law and order, feed people, restart basic public services, and generate local employment. Moreover, stabilization requires the reintegration of emigres, refugees, and soldiers returning from abroad. These are the actions that provide "security" to every member of a given society. That is the primary basis on which stabilization, popular allegiance to the state, and societal cohesion are built. At the same time, these are the essential elements that have to be in place to regenerate the economy.[4]

The third phase of a stabilization and responsible governance program is even more comprehensive than the second. Regenerating the economy and providing meaningful work and pay to individuals is fundamental. This need not lead to immediate prosperity but only to a reasonable hope for things to steadily improve. Providing meaningful work provides another strong sense of security and gives people a stake in the society and governing institutions. Therefore, socioeconomic safety nets for the unemployed, pensioners, and expatriates must be created to prevent social tensions from undermining the regeneration and modernization processes.[5]

The root cause factors that brought on the crisis of governance in the first place must also be addressed early in the socioeconomic transition process. Such factors include private exploitation of public and human resources, political exclusion, corruption, lack of health and education facilities, and degradation of the environment. These causes, and more, of poverty, disease, and violence are clearly understood to frustrate and obstruct political, economic, and social development. At the same time, it is understood that the sum of the parts of a desired countereffort to deal with major internal security threats requires more than regenerating the economy, dealing with root causes of instability, and preventing state failure. What is also required is the ability and willingness to exert effective, discrete, and deadly force against those individual men and women who are willing to violently exploit instability and state failure for their own ideological or personal enrichment purposes. However, for ultimate effectiveness and the requirement for rebuilding social cohesion, security forces must be required to deal with the violent internal opposition on the basis of the rule of law or its equivalent in a given polity.[6]

CULTIVATION OF A CIVIL SOCIETY

To begin with, the most important societal requirements necessary to build social cohesion are to enforce law and order, feed people, restart basic public services, generate local employment, and integrate immigrants and refugees into the general population. Within that context, popular perceptions of the moral rectitude of political leadership are key to rebuilding social cohesion and public confidence in government. In turn, popular perceptions depend on the proverbial transparency and accountability of government. As an example, a credible media is crucial to this process in order to help educate the population, reflect public opinion, and help keep government officials honest. With these building blocks in place, a legitimate civil society can become a real possibility.

The intent of all these is to generate the societal acceptance and support that governing institutions need to manage internal change and violence and to fairly and effectively guarantee individual and collective well-being.[7] This takes us back to where we started—that is, the stabilization process. Remember, stabilization is only one part of the circular and ever-improving process that defines, more than anything else, progress toward responsible governance and viable national security.

THE KIND OF POLITICAL DEVELOPMENT THAT LEADS TO RESPONSIBLE GOVERNANCE

Once the necessary internal conditions for peace and stability are established, only sustained cooperative work to deal with underlying economic, social, cultural, and humanitarian problems can place an enforced peace on durable foundations. Otherwise, it will be only a matter of time before a relapse into instability and conflict reoccurs. Thus, civilian and military leaders at all levels must understand the complete political-strategic nature of their tactical and operational actions. They must understand the ways by which force can be employed to achieve political and psychological as well as military ends. They must also understand the ways in which political and psychological considerations affect the use of force. They must also understand and deal with a diversity of organizations, peoples, and cultures, as well as with the local and global media. Lastly, they must understand how to cooperatively plan and implement interagency, international organization, nongovernmental organization, and coalition military operations. Most importantly, they must understand the centrality of rectitude and moral legitimacy.[8]

Critical points about moral legitimacy must be understood at three different levels. First, regime legitimacy is the primary target of the insurgents (or whatever term that might define internal adversaries). Second, a regime and its allies must protect and enhance culturally accepted moral legitimacy as the primary means by which that regime might survive. Third, a besieged government looking abroad for support against an internal foe, or to deny support to that adversary, must understand that rectitude and legitimacy is a double-edged moral sword. It will either assist or constrain foreign willingness and ability to become effectively involved. In sum, legitimacy is the central strategic problem in contemporary conflict. It is the hub of all powers and movements around which everything revolves. Popular perception of right and wrong, poverty, lack of upward mobility, and corruption threaten the right and the ability of any given regime to conduct the legitimizing functions of the state. These popular perceptions are empirically proven keys to the positive or negative outcome of contemporary conflict.[9]

VIGNETTE 1: A "NEW" CENTER OF GRAVITY: PUBLIC OPINION, POLITICAL LEADERSHIP, AND THE CENTRALITY OF MORAL LEGITIMACY—LESSONS FROM VIETNAM'S WAR FOR NATIONAL LIBERATION, 1959–1975

Introduction and Context

In rethinking of threat and response in the new global security environment, one must realize that the United States, Europe, and those other parts of the international community most integrated into the interdependent global economy are embroiled in a complex and ambiguous security arena. That arena, although possibly less bloody in soft-power terms, is ultimately based on some type of compulsion. Given this reality, failure to prepare adequately for present and future unconventional contingencies is unconscionable. The first cognitive step in developing an appropriate response to contemporary unconventional (i.e., asymmetric or hybrid) conflict is to become more aware of global disequilibrium and popular sovereignty. That would lead to a better understanding of the kind of war one is getting into and the circular relationship of security to legitimate governance. The second cognitive step is to realize, whether prepared for it or not, a populace-oriented model that most accurately describes the contemporary security arena. Taking these steps would set the foundation for a better understanding of and a more effective response to a nontraditional people-oriented asymmetric conflict.

Issue and Context Part One: A Little Bit of History

In 1959, the use of revolutionary violence to overthrow the French-supported South Vietnamese government in Saigon was approved at a Communist Party conference in North Vietnam. In 1960, the National Liberation Front (NLF or Vietcong) was organized to mobilize international and internal opposition (i.e., an insurgency) in the south. The United States introduced combat troops into the conflict in March 1965 after the French had withdrawn their forces from South Vietnam. Then, after the 1973 Accords negotiated with North Vietnam, the United States withdrew from the conflict. Saigon fell to regular North Vietnamese forces on April 30, 1975.[10]

This was only the most recent Vietnamese war for national liberation fought against foreign occupiers. The U.S. "neocolonialism" followed a 100-year-long series of conflicts against the Chinese, the French, the Japanese, and the French again after World War II. As a consequence, the will and capability to overcome foreign domination had been infused into four generations of Vietnamese. With that as political-psychological background, the unified NLF leadership made an analysis of the social situation and the balance of forces in order to (1) understand the nature of the conflict and validate an appropriate geopolitical end state, (2) determine and understand the primary centers of gravity that must be attacked and defended, (3) establish the fundamental operational-level tasks that must be undertaken to achieve the geostrategic end-state objectives, (4) understand the "strategic whole" of the conflict and establish the guiding principles for the conflict, and (5) develop a long-term overarching conceptual scheme (i.e., strategy or theory of engagement) from which to provide the guidance that would take the NLF to the geopolitical end-state solution to the conflict.

Thus, in 1959, well before the introduction of the U.S. combat forces into the Vietnamese conflict, the NLF was organizing to mobilize and train to conduct a media war and a conventional insurgency in what was then called South Vietnam. At the same time, a cadre of well-educated civilian and military planners and practitioners was organized in order to begin the development of a core of strategic leaders who would actually conduct the war against the legitimacy of the corrupt and foreign-dominated South Vietnamese government.

In turn, the party leadership created and began to employ well-disciplined and highly motivated insurgent forces that (1) adopted the strategy and tactics of a war of the weak against the strong; (2) was capable of discrete, rapid, and decisive surgical operations anywhere in the battlespace; and (3) was designed to achieve political, psychological, and military objectives—in that order. Thus, as early as 1959, the party leadership began to plan for and undertake a general insurgency war that was combined with a political-psychological legitimacy war. Those wars were supported by media and diplomatic wars that specifically targeted the legitimacy of the South Vietnamese government. Those wars also attacked the U.S. and international public opinion and generated considerable support for Vietnam all around the world.

In sum, this combination of political-psychological-military efforts was organized and carefully orchestrated over a long period of time by a united political party. The NLF understood that this kind of people-centric effort would be a powerful force multiplier and facilitator in the global security arena. That concept, in the Vietnam War and elsewhere, worked on two levels—offensive and defensive. On the offensive level, a protagonist can develop positive power well beyond his own capabilities. On the defensive level, one can take indirect and direct measures to deprive the enemy of significant external and internal support and gain a relative advantage. What happened was that the U.S. and South Vietnamese forces would conduct a series of highly effective military operations that forced the Vietcong and their North Vietnamese allies to withdraw from the immediate battlefield. Yet, despite successive traditional defeats, the insurgents kept coming back. They kept coming back from different directions, and they were always refreshed, resupplied, and rededicated. Eventually, of course, they prevailed. Colonel Harry G. Summers captured the situation beautifully: "You know you never defeated us on the battlefield." The North Vietnamese colonel pondered this remark a moment. "That may be so," he replied, "but it is also irrelevant."[11]

Issue and Context Part Two: A Populist-Oriented Model

Carl von Clausewitz's a priori "remarkable trinity" is a populace-oriented model that is remarkably similar to the SWORD peace-security paradigm. It depicts the activities and efforts of the most important players involved in a given security arena. That trinity includes the following: (1) the people, (2) the government, and (3) the civil-military commander in chief. First, that model portrays the allegiance of a population as the primary center of gravity. The kind of persuasive, co-optive, and coercive measures taken by a regime and its opposition will determine success or failure of one party or the other in the achievement of expected socioeconomic-political development, a just civil society, responsible governance, and a sustainable peace. Thus, both the government and its allies and the belligerent opposition and its allies can coerce, persuade, and convince the populace that they will make the most legitimate efforts to ensure personal security, development, and well-being. Second, the primary aim of both the government and the violent opposition is to undertake direct and indirect political, economic, social, psychological, and security programs and actions (i.e., a whole-of-government or multi-dimensional hybrid approach) to shift popular opinion in their respective favor. And, again, in Clausewitzian and empirical terms, the people and their allegiance is the key center of gravity in contemporary conflict. Third, in contemporary war, the military and its commander must give way to the civil-military commander in chief who can conduct a unified whole-of-government—plus international partners—effort. Clausewitz would remind us one more time that the grand strategic objective would be to shift popular support in one's respective favor. Accordingly, the primary center of gravity changes from a familiar conventional military-centric concept to a more ambiguous populace-oriented paradigm. Interestingly, that "new" center of gravity was articulated about 200 years ago.[12]

These points are all too relevant to the "new" political-psychological conflicts of the twenty-first century. Qiao Liang and Wang Xiangsui remind us once again that a kinder, gentler war in which bloodshed and brutality may be reduced is still a war. "It may alter some of the bloody processes of war, but there is no way to change the essence of war, which is one of compulsion, and therefore it cannot alter its cruel outcome either."[13]

Findings

If the lessons from the Vietnam experience teach us anything, they teach us that there are other, more effective, ways and means to "render the enemy powerless" than to attack his military force.[14] One of Clausewitz's translators, Michael Howard, reminds us that the most refined tactical doctrine, operational expertise, and logistical skills that are carried out by optimum military structure in pursuit of a policy that ignores the strategic whole—the populace, the government, as well as the military—will be irrelevant.[15]

Outcomes

Tactically, except for shows of force, the Vietcong insurgents operated in relatively small units with political, psychological, and military objectives—again, in that order. "Armed propaganda" was conducted not to "win" but to discredit the South Vietnamese government and the Americans. At the same time, "armed propaganda" was intended to keep the United States off balance and frustrated. It was also intended to give the country and the world the impression that the Vietcong was more powerful than it really was. Operationally, the insurgents expanded political, military, and support components and consolidated their de facto legitimacy position with the "masses." The overarching purpose of all these tactical and operational activities was to demonstrate to the Vietnamese people and to the world that the inept and corrupt incumbent regime in Saigon was unwilling and unable to perform its legitimizing security and service functions. The strategic purpose of the Vietcong and their Vietnamese sponsors was to conduct a populace-oriented political-psychological struggle over the moral right to govern the entire country. These indirect attacks were generally aimed at societal grievances such as political and economic injustice, racial and religious discrimination, debilitating internal corruption, and unwelcome foreign domination. The South Vietnamese and their American ally never really addressed these issues. The dominant Americans were intent on winning a localized military war of attrition.[16]

Then, as noted earlier, when it finally became obvious that the conventional military war against the Vietcong and its North Vietnamese ally was a failure, the United States entered into negotiations that would allow the peaceful withdrawal of its military forces from Vietnam. After the Paris Accords of 1973, the North Vietnamese waited for a diplomatically prudent period of time and, in 1975, actions were taken that led to the following: (1) the quick defeat in detail of the South Vietnamese army, (2) the fall of Saigon, (3) the unconditional capitulation of the South Vietnamese government, and (4) the final unification of the Vietnamese nation. All these were achieved as a result of the careful planning and implementation of the effort that began 16 years earlier in 1959.[17]

Conclusions and Implications

Victory in any kind of conflict situation is not simply the sum of the battles won over the course of a conflict. Rather, it is the product of connecting and weighting the various elements of national and international power within the context of strategic appraisals, strategic objectives, and strategic clarity. Together, properly prepared leadership and organization at the highest levels can determine and pursue long-term and short-term mutually supportive objectives. Without leaders and organization that can establish, enforce, and continually refine a holistic plan and generate consistent national and international support, authority is fragmented and ineffective and there is no strategic clarity. Without strategic clarity, there is little hope for resolving the myriad problems endemic to a lack of unity of effort (i.e., strategic clarity) in contemporary conflict. Thus, the result is failure and the aftermath of failure.[18]

KEY POINTS AND LESSONS

Key Points

Conflict (i.e., war) has changed. The aim is not so much to kill people or bomb war-making capabilities but to sap the ability and will of an adversary. Practitioners of contemporary asymmetric hybrid war act in accordance with a political logic that is the continuation of politics through the use of co-optive and coercive political-psychological persuasion. The common denominator motive in this equation is a willingness to induce radical political-economic-social change in a targeted society.

- All of that is intended to capture the imaginations of the people (i.e., the new center of gravity) and harness the will of their leaders. Thus, the struggle is total in that it gives the winner the absolute power to control or replace an existing government or other symbol of power.
- The threat, then, is not an enemy military force or even the debilitating instability generated by a violent asymmetric aggressor. At base, the threat is the inability or unwillingness of a government to prevent the compulsion of radical change and/or protect its people from a violent imposition of radical political-economic-social restructuring of the state.
- The power to deal effectively with this kind of threat does not lie in hard military firepower or police power. Instead, the power to deal with this threat involves a whole-of-government approach that can apply the full human and physical resources of a nation-state and its international partners to achieve

the personal and collective security and well-being that leads to development and responsible governance.

- Thus, as noted in other cases, the principal tools of statecraft have changed from reactive military-police confrontation to the proactive use of words, images, symbols, perceptions, and ideas aimed at public opinion and leadership.
- War will not disappear from the face of the earth. It only changes.

Lessons

In the chaotic contemporary security environment, leaders of international organizations, governments, security forces, and other institutions responsible for collective and personal security and well-being find themselves in a quandary. They have tended to ignore or wish away threats perpetrated by nonstate actors such as the Vietcong. They do not know what to do or how to do it.

VIGNETTE 2: THE WAR FOR ALGERIAN INDEPENDENCE, 1954–1962

Introduction

The concept of whole-of-government and international partner activities is closely related to the notion of combinations. The idea is to use all available instruments of power in modern conflict situations and target public opinion as the primary center of gravity. As we continue to repeat, the methodology of contemporary war is no longer based on a singular military-centric paradigm. Clausewitz recognized that issue in three different contexts. First, his "Remarkable Trinity" of governing elements in war includes the populace, the government, and the military. Thus, we address the whole-of-government unity of effort. Second, Clausewitz understood that military- and people-centric war is the continuation of politics by other means and it should be directed by the highest governmental authority. That commander in chief would be expected to use combinations of all available domestic and foreign instruments of statecraft in pursuing the grand strategic political objective of the effort. In these terms, "it is possible to increase the likelihood of success without defeating the enemy's (military) forces." Third, the great man taught that in internal as well as external conflicts the center of gravity is leadership and public opinion.[19]

Context

The central idea in contemporary conflict is to influence and then control people and their values (i.e., the human terrain rather than the geographical terrain). The purpose of combinations is threefold: (1) combinations can generate a system of offensive and defensive power that is a great force multiplier, (2) combinations of instruments of statecraft force an adversary to fight on multiple fronts that are determined by the opponent's strengths and weaknesses, and (3) any given combination of powers can be designed specifically to force the erosion of an adversary's morale and will to resist or to protect one's own primary center of gravity.

As a consequence, the hard-won lessons of the past and present demonstrate the following two closely related phenomena: (1) the winner is the political actor who best combines the instruments of power at his or her disposal with (2) the intent to capture the will of a people and their leaders. The dominating characteristic of a war of this kind can be defined as military, political, economic, informational, cultural, or technical. Then, each type of war may be subdivided into subparts. For example, military war can be organized into land, sea, air, cyber, space, electronic, and chemical-biological. Economic war can be divided into trade, financial, sanctions, and so on. At the same time, every type of war can be combined with as many others as a protagonist's imagination, organization, and resources can manage. As an example, empirical data dictate that military war must be strongly supported by media (i.e., informational/cultural) war and a combination of other types of war that might include but are not limited to psychological war, financial war, cyber war, or diplomatic war. The only limitation is one's imagination.

The Algerian case illustrates the empirical reality of the beginning of the end of purely military-oriented conflicts and the beginning of the use of a multidimensional approach (i.e., hybrid combinations) of modern unconventional war. This case also shows us that war has become a juxtaposition of disparate but highly interrelated actions (i.e., dimensions). The combined power of diplomacy, intelligence, ruse, media (propaganda), cultural manipulation, and physical coercion (i.e., armed propaganda) has succeeded the limited power of the "shock and awe" of conventional maneuver warfare. Thus, the Algerian war for independence is one more confirmation of the notion that the concepts of "enemy" and the conventional military center of gravity have drastically changed and the ways and means of attacking an opponent infinitely broadened.

In Algeria, the stage was set for an attempt at revolution early in the twentieth century. It was organized by a puritanical Islamic sect that called for a total rejection of European culture and physical isolation from the French. As such, the revolution of the 1950s and early 1960s was not something that came out of the desires and needs of the peasantry and proletariat. And, it was not something that represented the Algerian people's deepest ideological concerns. The resistance to French rule from about 1830 to 1940 was conducted almost exclusively in the name of religion—not nationalism. The resistance to French rule after World War II, however, was orchestrated and led by a small group of middle-class nationalist intellectuals and politicians.[20]

Findings: The Grand Strategy for the Algerian Revolutionary War

Historian Matthew Connelly argues that the origins of the grand strategy for the Algerian War for Independence can be traced to the last days of World War II. Nationalists all over the world, including Algerians, had associated themselves with American anticolonialism and organized celebratory marches. Many of these, including the Algerian marches, quickly turned into clashes with colonial forces in which, for example, the French reportedly killed from 6,000 to 45,000 Algerians. In turn, Algeria's leading opposition figure, Messali Hadj, created a political party—the Movement for the Triumph of Democratic Liberties (*Mouvement pour la Triomphe des Libertes Democratiques*, MTLD). The party won municipal elections all across Algeria, but in subsequent elections that were held in 1948, the French arrested MTLD candidates and stuffed ballot boxes in favor of their "Muslim yes-men."

Later that year, the MTLD asked the head of its paramilitary section, Hocine Ait Ahmed, to advise the party on how it might win Algeria's independence through the use of armed force. He studied previous examples and the insights of thinkers such as Sun Tzu, Clausewitz, and Liddell Hart and came to the conclusion that the use of armed force could not succeed against the French Army in Algeria. Alternatively, Ait Ahmed recommended a strategy that would coordinate a combination of insurgency war, psychological war, media war, and diplomatic war. The primary effort, however, would be a diplomatic war of national liberation. The MTLD approved the report in December 1948. The younger more radical militants were not particularly happy with a strategy that reduced the use of armed force to a supporting guerrilla role. As a consequence, they created an opposition party—the *Front de Liberation Nationale* (National Liberation Front [FLN]). In 1954, that organization forced the MTLD to give the conventional, "more romantic," military approach to revolution the same status as the diplomatic component of the war for national liberation. This was just fine as far as the MTLD and Ait Ahmed were concerned. A strong military dimension of the conflict would divert the attention of the French public, the army, and the government from the primary political-psychological thrust of the revolutionary effort. It would also divide the French public opinion and the political leadership. In these terms, the addition of a stronger military dimension did in fact divert attention from the nonkinetic dimensions of the conflict and generated a situation in which the disunited French nation could not develop a viable counterrevolutionary effort.

In the meantime, the Algerian revolutionary leadership appears to have agreed that the major thrust of the conflict would have to be a global information war for public opinion. Ait Ahmed's program for diplomatic war, then, was to ensure that the psychological, information, and military components of the whole diplomatic campaign were mutually reinforcing and were communicated effectively all around the world. And, despite military defeat at the hands of the French Army, the unifying diplomatic, psychological, and informational elements of the revolutionary strategy kept the fragmented Algerians relatively better unified than the French. That led to the Evian Accords of March 1962 and Algerian national independence on July 4, 1962.[21]

Outcome: The French Response

France's Fourth Republic, which lasted until General Charles de Gaulle took power in 1958 and created the Fifth Republic, was handicapped by its parliamentary and electoral systems. These systems favored multiple political parties and produced unstable coalition governments. During the whole period of its tenure after the end of World War II, the Fourth Republic averaged a new government every eight months. Moreover, just before the promulgation of the Fifth Republic, France's third government in 11 months resigned on April 15, 1958. The political instability and governmental inertia in the period after the end of World War II caused, as only a few examples, the loss of two-thirds of France's currency reserves, growth in foreign debt, increase in budget deficits, and chronic inflation. Clearly, the French economy and the French people had not been served well by its political system. Likewise, French troops participating in the colonial wars after the end of the world war had been well served by the Fourth Republic and were beginning to exhibit mutinous attitudes toward France's political leadership. Additionally, Algeria had a large European population that exercised considerable political power in the French parliament and was the cause of government deadlocks on more than a few occasions. Thus, the political, economic, social, and military disarray in postwar France generated a situation in which neither the government nor the army could develop a viable ideology, strategy, organization, or the discipline necessary to mount an effective counter-insurgency effort in Algeria.

Nevertheless, by the end of 1957, the French Army had almost completely ejected FLN forces from the large cities and towns of Algeria and had effectively interrupted transit between the Algerian revolutionaries and their external support. Some of the methods used in achieving those objectives, however, were unconscionable. Those methods included sequestration in concentration camps and villages, raids of retribution on Muslim villages, execution of hostages, summary trials, executions, and "torture methods of which the Gestapo would have been envious." As a result, the French Army alienated much of the Algerian population, French public opinion at home and abroad, and world opinion and leadership. Algerian international and public diplomacy and information campaigns at home and abroad were provided material that could not have been made up even by the world's best fiction writers. It was only a matter of time before everyone in the global community clearly understood that French moral rectitude was deficient and the revolutionary alternative was far superior. As a consequence, even though the French had destroyed the FLN's conventional military capability by 1962, Algerian political independence was achieved by a strategy that aimed at establishing a mutually reinforcing relationship between the diplomatic and political-psychological campaign abroad and media informational efforts to generate popular support at home and abroad.[22]

Conclusions

The uncomfortable reality of contemporary asymmetric, hybrid war is that it is now a vast interlocking system of combinations of instruments of statecraft that can be used to overthrow the established authority in a country. In view of the present-day interdependence of the global community, any residual grievance within a targeted geographical or human terrain, no matter how localized and lacking in scope, can be brought into the framework of the contemporary global war for public opinion. Thus, in this context, it is crucial to remember that a combination of indirect power instruments applied many thousands of miles away from Algeria to Europe, America, and the Far East turned out to be far more decisive than the military-centric efforts executed in Algeria.

KEY POINTS AND LESSONS

Key Points

The Algerian War for National Independence is instructive in many ways. The most important, however, should probably include the following:

- Algeria is a classic case study in the value of combinations of nonkinetic as well as kinetic approaches to contemporary conflict.
- Algeria was the first case in the post–World War II era to clearly demonstrate that political-military leaders at all levels must understand how political-psychological considerations can be employed as effective nonlethal means of persuasion and coercion.

- The Algerian case explicitly and implicitly shows that combinations of the various political-psychological instruments of statecraft are strong force multipliers in contemporary hybrid conflict.

- Modern asymmetric wars, such as that demonstrated in Algeria, is not a test of expertise in creating instability, killing enemies, conducting unconscionable violence, or achieving political, commercial, ideological, or moral satisfaction. It is a zero-sum game and, thus, it is an exercise in survival.

- If we are to succeed in dealing with the hybrid confrontations and conflicts we now face, we must adapt our cognitive approaches and organize our institutions to the "new" realities noted earlier. This is the indispensable lesson from the Algerian War for Independence.

Lessons

Finally, contemporary nontraditional war is not a kind of appendage—a lesser or limited thing—to the conventional concept of conflict. It is a great deal more. As long as an opposition exists that is willing to risk all to violently take down a government and establish its own, there is war. This, again, is a zero-sum game in which there is only one winner. It is, thus, total. In the *Centurions*, Larteguy vividly captures the difference between traditional warfare designed to achieve limited political, economic, or territorial concessions and the totality of the type of conflict we confront today. He contrasts the traditional French and the unconventional total methods of waging contemporary conflict.

It is difficult to explain exactly, but it is rather like (the card game) bridge as compared to *belote*. When we (the French) make war, we play *belote* with 32 cards in the pack. But the Viet Minh's game is bridge and they have 52 cards: 20 more than we do. Those 20 cards short will always prevent us from getting the better of them. They've got nothing to do with traditional (military) warfare, they're marked with the sign of politics, propaganda, faith, agrarian reform. ... What's biting the French officer? I think he is beginning to realize that we've got to play with 52 cards and he doesn't like it at all ... those 20 extra cards aren't at all to his liking.[23]

Total war is not a test of expertise in creating instability, achieving some sort of moral satisfaction, or getting a higher body count than an adversary. Ultimately, once again, it is an exercise in survival. Failure in contemporary total conflict is not an option. These are the realities for now and in to the rest of the century. Everything else is illusion.

Governance and Sovereignty: The British Experience in Malaya (1948–1960) and Some Contrasting Lessons from El Salvador (1979–1992)

During the time when the Peace of Westphalia (1648) was being negotiated and before Jean-Jacques Rousseau wrote *The Social Contract* (1789), Thomas Hobbes introduced the political problem of governance. He argued that Westphalia would be the catalyst that would tear down the notion of the divine right of kings to act as the sovereign "Vicars of God" on the earth. He also explained that there must be some coercive power to replace that which was being torn down—that is, there must be some power capable of protecting a people from foreign invasion and the lawlessness of fellow citizens. Without a *Leviathan* (i.e., commonwealth or sovereign power) to punish wrong, prevent the chaos of local and global anarchy, and provide for the general well-being, life would be "nasty, brutish, and short."[1]

Hobbes also contended that weak regimes lose moral legitimacy over time. The loss of moral legitimacy leads to a degeneration of de facto and de jure sovereignty. In any event, that leaves a vacuum in which all kinds of nonstate and state actors can contribute substantially to the process of state failure. State and/or nonstate actors have been known to step into that vacuum and create something else that contributes to their own specific interests. As a consequence, millions of people become emigrants or refugees or die. This reality translates into security challenges that strategic leaders must face now and in the future. They must be prepared to think about these issues from the perspective of governance and public opinion as the central strategic problem of this time in history. They must be prepared to think about these problems from different perspectives and at different levels. They must also be prepared to deal with legitimate governance as the most important issue in dealing with the totality of contemporary multidimensional conflict. Otherwise, Hobbes would warn us again that life would be "nasty, brutish, and short."[2]

To help clarify the general relationship between legitimate governance and sovereignty and the more specific issues that contribute to the definition, understanding, and relationship of responsible governance to sovereignty, we look to the following: (1) the relationship of responsible governance to sovereignty, (2) the architecture for a foundation of moral legitimacy, (3) the circular nature and interrelationship of the components of the security-peace paradigm, and (4) the need to "nurture" moral legitimacy. Then, the first accompanying vignette reviews the exemplary British approach to the problem of insurgency and governance in Malaya, 1949–1960—that is, the "spiraling up" from colony status to a legitimate nation-state. The second vignette reviews the anything but exemplary American approach to insurgency and governance in El Salvador, 1978–1992—that is, the "spiraling down" from responsible governance to failing state status and its aftermath.

THE RELATIONSHIP OF RESPONSIBLE GOVERNANCE TO SOVEREIGNTY

The evolutionary result of Hobbes's thinking was more fully expressed over a hundred years later in 1762, with Rousseau's *The Social Contract*, and the American Constitution of 1789. These documents set forth the concept of popular sovereignty. Rousseau taught the Western world that the ultimate purpose of a government was to interpret and enforce "the general (the people's) will." The U.S. Constitution speaks of "We the People." Then, over the next 200 years, the evolutionary process of international law has worked to bring together the principles of protection of people and prevention of egregious harm to people and the notion of responsible governance. With that, state sovereignty has become conditional. The individual sovereign or the assembly (i.e., parliament, congress, legislature, or chamber of deputies) of citizens must do more in governance than protecting the polity from foreign invaders, providing internal law and order, and defining the general will. The sovereign state must also concern itself with the manner of governance as well as the fact of governing.

Now, more and more, legitimate governance is defined as governance that generates a viable political competence that (1) can and will effectively manage, coordinate, and sustain personal and collective security and (2) can and will effectively generate political, economic, and social development with moral rectitude. The operative term here is "rectitude." This depends on the culture and mores of the community of citizens being governed. Moral legitimacy and responsible sovereignty are, then, becoming synonymous and ultimately defined by public opinion and the concept of the "hearts and minds" of the populace. As a consequence, without the guarantee of responsible and competent state-administered control of the national territory and the people in it, every other form of sovereignty/security is likely to remain elusive.[3]

THE ARCHITECTURE FOR A FOUNDATION OF MORAL LEGITIMACY

Empirical data show that there are five basic indicators (i.e., independent variables) of moral legitimacy that must be implemented by virtually any political actor facing the nontraditional and traditional threats and internal violence inherent in the current global disequilibrium. These variables are not new in discussions dealing with the idea of state legitimacy. As noted earlier, they reflect traditional theoretical concepts closely associated with the classical political-philosophical notion of popular sovereignty articulated in the U.S. Constitution and by John Locke, John Stuart Mill, and Rousseau. As noted in Chapter 1, this security-peace model as a whole is statistically significant at the 0.001 level and predicts at an impressive 88 percent of the win/loss results of the 69 cases examined. The most salient independent variables defining the legitimacy dimension of the model are derived from a *probit* analysis of the data. What is new is, first, the specific combination of variables considered to be the most powerful indicators of legitimacy. Second, the interdependence of these variables has not often been stressed in the international politics literature. Third, the interdependence of the legitimacy dimension with the other principal components of the general legitimate governance peace-security paradigm has not been stressed. Fourth, these variables can be used as objective measures of effectiveness at the macro level for winning or losing in the contemporary conflict arena. Remember, this model was not conceived a priori. It was developed empirically and warrants confidence that the findings are universal and explain most of the reality of the contemporary global security environment.

As noted in Chapter 1, the five independent variables that explain and define the legitimizing and strengthening of the state are as follows: (1) free, fair, and frequent *selection* of leaders; (2) the level of participation in or acceptance of the political process; (3) the level of governmental corruption; (4) the level of security and concomitant political-economic-social development; and (5) the level of regime acceptance by major social institutions. These key indicators and measures of moral legitimacy are not exhaustive, but they statistically explain a high percentage of the legitimacy phenomenon and provide the basic architecture for the actions necessary to assist governments in their struggle to survive, develop, and prosper. As such, these indicators constitute a strong coherent conceptual framework (i.e., the security-peace paradigm) from which policy, strategy, and operational efforts might flow. The paradigm is equally valid for policy makers of threatened states, as well as nonstate entities interested in taking down a given regime—that is, the degree to which a political actor effectively manages a balanced mix of these independent variables that enables stability, development, political competence, security, acceptance, and sustainable peace—or the reverse.[4]

THE CIRCULAR NATURE OF THE SECURITY-PEACE PARADIGM

Clearly, these independent variables are the pragmatic foundations for national and global well-being. These variables are also the fundamental elements that define the social contract between a people and their government. Leaders who understand this also understand that these closely related variables operate in a circular pattern—again, that is, peace and security, stability and development, responsible governance and effective sovereignty, and back again to peace and security. This circular pattern seems to take us around and around, again and again. To be more than temporarily effective, however, the circular nature of the peace-security equation requires the development of an upward (positive) spiral. Security also depends on the continuing and expanding development of a country's socioeconomic-political infrastructure. Within this context, a morally honest and competent governing regime can and must generate a continuing and improving upward spiral moving toward a higher and better level of peace and security. Otherwise, with no improvement in personal and collective well-being and relatively no socioeconomic-political development, a situation is created that would be, in fact, a downward and negative movement toward state failure and its aftermath.[5]

NURTURING LEGITIMATE GOVERNANCE

The achievement of the objectives noted earlier requires the nurturing of responsible governance. That requires the capturing of the proverbial hearts and minds of the peoples involved. That, in turn, would require the application of the five independent variables noted earlier. To repeat, they are as follows: (1) the generation of a high level of popular participation in the political process, (2) a concerted anticorruption and public diplomacy effort, (3) a steadily improving level of political-economic-social development, (4) a high level of regime acceptance by major social institutions, (5) a high level of public acceptance of the reforms necessary to manage the multidimensional root causes of instability and violence, and (6) dealing appropriately with the wars within the war. These are the bases from which to secure the hearts and minds of the populace and develop and protect one's own center of gravity. These are also the pragmatic foundations for national well-being and stability and the fundamental elements that give a regime the moral right to govern.[6]

No group or force can simply legislate or decree these measures for itself. It must develop, sustain, and enhance them by its own actions over time. Again, as noted elsewhere, legitimization and internal stability derive from popular and institutional perceptions that authority is genuine and effective and uses morally correct means for reasonable and fair purposes. Moreover, the evidence from over 70 wars in the late twentieth and early twenty-first centuries shows that when all five independent variables are applied in a strong and dynamic manner, the probability of success is increased. Conversely, when some of the indicators are applied in an ad hoc, piecemeal, or unbalanced manner, the probability of failure is increased.[7]

All this does not mean that the United States or any other power must be involved in everything at all times. That is impossible. As also noted elsewhere, the general rule would be that decision makers and policymakers must carefully examine the social engineering problem and calculate the possible and the impossible and the gains and losses. Then, when the case warrants, they should intervene earlier rather than later. If done earlier, the initial and intense use of low-cost diplomatic and nonkinetic resources and military support units can be utilized to ensure legitimacy and stability. If done later, the initial and intense use of high-cost kinetic resources will generally be applied to a losing situation. Ultimately, however, Ambassador George Kennan reminds us that the only test for involvement—whatever its form and level—is national self-interest—that is, again, the only morality within the anarchy of world disorder.[8]

VIGNETTE 1: FIVE QUICK LESSONS FROM MALAYA, 1948–1960

Introduction and Context

Critical points about moral legitimacy (i.e., responsible sovereignty) must be understood at four levels. They are as follows: (1) regime legitimacy is the primary target of a nonstate or state actor attempting to compel or persuade a targeted regime to accept its will; (2) a regime and its allies must protect and enhance moral legitimacy as the primary means by which that regime might improve itself and survive; (3) a besieged government looking abroad for support against an internal foe—or to deny support to that adversary—must understand that rectitude and legitimacy is a double-edged sword that will either assist or constrain foreign willingness and ability to become effectively involved in any given internal conflict; and (4) only sustained, cooperative work to deal with underlying political, economic, and social problems can place an achieved peace on a durable foundation and avoid an eventual relapse back into conflict. Otherwise, internal reform and peace operations risk becoming little more than limited and unsuccessful military occupations.

Findings and Outcome

The Malayan case is a clear-cut example of a well-organized and well-executed long-term effort to counter an insurgency and become the type of regime that can and will achieve legitimate nation-state status. The main point of this exercise is to demonstrate that the protagonist who will succeed in this type of conflict is the one who best understands and applies moral legitimacy as the primary operational-level means by which he might fight and survive. These kinds of confrontations cannot rely only on infantry, tanks, and aircraft to attack the enemy strategy. This kind of conflict must rely primarily on words, images, perceptions, ideas, and soft power to achieve its ends. Thus, the challenge for those who must plan and conduct the various wars within the general asymmetric war is to come to an agreement on a clear grand geostrategic political objective (i.e., end state). Then, the task would be to plan and implement a unified operational-level effort to achieve that strategic-level end. Together, these integrating and legitimizing efforts can establish the kind of stability and well-being that is derived from popular perceptions that a given regime's authority is reasonable and culturally appropriate.

Lessons from the Malayan Emergency

General Sir Robert Thompson (Ret., UK) has outlined five highly related basic and positive principles that governed the exemplary British approach to the post–World War II Malayan Emergency, 1948–1960.

The first principle is that the government must have a clear grand strategic geopolitical aim—that is, to establish and maintain a free, independent, and united country that is politically, economically, and socially stable and viable. The intent is fourfold: (1) there would be strategic clarity (i.e., a complete unity of effort); (2) there would be no "dirty war"; (3) there would be no short-term ad hocery and mission creep; and (4) most importantly, there would be a workable, practical, and viable end-state transition policy that would take the British out of Malaya and transfer governance to a free, independent, united, and politically capable country that would be politically, economically, socially, and militarily stable and viable. This, of course, would not be a quick and easy fix, but General Thompson understood that to be far superior to the intolerably wasteful and costly alternatives.[9]

The second principle addressed the moral right of a regime to govern. This concept is critical in an internal war. The threat of an adversary's program relies on grievances such as political-economic-social injustices as the means through which to indirectly attack a government. The political leadership, civil bureaucracy, and the security organizations of a targeted state must understand that popular perceptions of various injustices tend to limit the right—and the ability—of a government to conduct the business of state. Additionally, the political leadership, civil bureaucracy, and security forces must attain the mentality to engage adversaries without unnecessarily alienating the citizenry.

The third principle takes us back to the first and second principles. The targeted government must have an overall plan detailing how and with what resources (i.e., the ways and means) it will achieve its ultimate strategic geopolitical objective. This plan cannot be narrowly military centric. It must include all political, economic, social, informational, administrative, police, and other "whole-of-government" measures that have a bearing on the conflict. Above all, it must clearly define roles and responsibilities to avoid duplication of effort and to ensure that there are no gaps in a balanced, multidimensional, people-centric effort. This is the coordinating mechanism that can avoid strategic ambiguity and reinforce the upward spiral moving toward the achievement of a grand geopolitical end state.

The fourth principle is closely related to the preceding principle—that is, the government must give priority to defeating the root causes of the political subversion, not a given violent politicized human enemy. The problem here is to isolate the enemy politically, psychologically, and militarily from its primary sources of aid and support. Accordingly, the Malayan insurgents were isolated from the rest of the community as a result of the efforts of the government and its security organizations functioning within the confines of the rule of law (i.e., the legitimacy war). The rule of law also dictated the conduct of the information war, the intelligence war, the creation of strategic hamlets, and the physical paramilitary war. As in other cases, the separation from the outside world generated by these various "wars within the war" caused the Malayan insurgents to withdraw more and more into their own compartmentalized and isolated organizational and support structures. That isolation precluded them from recruiting new membership and significantly reduced their ability to organize and execute meaningful actions. By the end of the "emergency," the insurgents' isolation had become nearly complete. Given the isolation of the insurgents, the government could more easily concentrate its efforts on the root cause problems that generated the insurgency in the first place. Additionally, and in those terms, great care was taken to be sensitive and accommodating to the general public throughout the entire 12-year process of finding, isolating, and neutralizing the insurgents.

General Thompson's fifth principle is that in the early phase of the insurgency, a targeted government must secure its base areas first. His logic and reasoning are interesting and important. The base areas contain the greatest number of the population and other resources vital to winning a conflict. The base areas also provide the space from which to work methodically outward in a "stream-roller" and "clear and hold" approach toward the general conflict. That, in turn, provides the people with palpable evidence of ultimate victory. This approach to an insurgency, then, does not require a large, expensive, and unwieldy military structure. The requirement is to create a small, elite, highly disciplined, highly mobile, and aggressive civil-military organization that can fulfill its proper security role in support of the civil authority. Then, with the obvious erosion of the insurgents' capabilities, people can begin to willingly provide intelligence. The short-term effect of improving human intelligence would be finding, discrediting, and neutralizing a given adversary. The long-term effect would be the shifting of the balance of power toward the legitimate branches of the Malayan government. This last principle ensures that all governmental civil-military efforts throughout the conflict would focus on "spiraling up" to one common objective—that is, creating, maintaining, and strengthening a legitimate Malaysian state.[10]

KEY POINTS AND LESSONS

Key Points

- The five principles aforementioned constitute the basis for a pragmatic and realistic approach to contemporary conflict and the manner of responsible governance.
- The argument against this approach is that it is too complicated, takes too long, and is too expensive.
- Strong empirical evidence, however, suggests that trying to do something less complicated, less time consuming, and less expensive actually takes a good deal more time, money, and effort than expected.
- The empirical evidence also indicates that the cost in terms of lives is inordinately expensive.

The Concluding Lessons

The British experience in Malaya demonstrates that the problem of governance is the central strategic problem and key to success or failure in modern asymmetric (i.e., hybrid) war. Like many other post–World War

II conflicts, the decolonization-governance problem in Malaya centered on popular perceptions of social justice and the moral right of the regime in power to conduct the business of the state. As a result, Malayan nationalist and politically left-oriented insurgents mobilized and conducted a classical Leninist-Maoist strategy to overthrow the British colonial state. When the British realized that the costs of militarily holding its former colony would be too high and would in any event lead to defeat, they planned, organized, and implemented an integrated and legitimizing political-military effort. That effort would establish and maintain a free, independent, and united country that would be politically, economically, and socially stable and viable. General Thompson would argue that that balanced effort was not an exit strategy. It was a transition strategy that would take 12 years to accomplish. It would, however, be far superior and considerably less costly than the intolerable murderous alternatives.[11]

This is nothing radical. It is basic security policy and national asset management. And, when we speak of legitimacy, we speak of legitimate governance. The distinguished French philosopher, Jacques Maritain, like many of his classical predecessors, argues that the state is an instrument in the service of man. "The highest functions of the State (are to) ensure the law and facilitate the free development of the body politic. Then only will the State achieve its true dignity, which comes not from power and prestige, but from the exercise of justice."[12] Thus, legitimate governance is more than de facto or de jure legitimacy. Legitimate governance concerns the manner of governing rather than the fact of governing.

VIGNETTE 2: THE SALVADORAN INSURGENCY

Introduction

The case of El Salvador represents a Chinese (Maoist) model of guerrilla war made popular in Latin America and elsewhere around the world by the charismatic Ernesto "Che" Guevara. This case also illustrates the difference between the American and the British responses to contemporary insurgency. Che Guevara took exception to the wisdom of Lenin and the experience of the Algerians. He argued that an insurrection, in itself, would create the conditions necessary to take down a targeted regime. The revolutionaries in Malaya also accepted the very similar "revolution comes from the barrel of a gun" strategy of Mao Tse-Tung. Such a revolution could be conducted by relatively small but mobile groups of guerrilla fighters.[13] A targeted government's inability to nullify the insurgents would force it to overreact against the insurgents and in so doing would begin to alienate the people. The insurgents would, then, act as a catalyst to challenge the legitimacy of the incumbent government and initiate popular support for the "revolution."[14] In Malaya, the British responded with a carefully coordinated multidimensional military-social-economic-political-psychological-intelligence strategy. Moreover, the British stayed in Malaysia until reforms were solidified and the country had developed a well-functioning economy and responsible governance. In El Salvador the Americans responded with a generally singular military-reformist strategy. Then, when the "war" was over, the Americans declared victory and went home. Today, El Salvador is one of the poorest, most corrupt, and dangerous places in the world. Malaysia, on the other hand, is doing relatively well.

Context

In the 1970s, chronic political, economic, and social problems created by a self-serving military-supported oligarchy began to generate another crisis in a long list of historical political crises in El Salvador. During that time, General Carlos Humberto Romero came to power with support of those who thought he would be able to establish a regime strong enough to protect the interests of the oligarchy and to control the various forces agitating for reform. Yet, by 1979, the situation was beyond control by repression.

The catalyst that ignited the violence in El Salvador was the military coup of October 1979 that ousted Romero as the last protector of the interests of the oligarchy. After Romero, the history of the country breaks down into four clearly defined periods. First, the period immediately after the coup was one of almost complete disarray. None of the three major actors in the conflict—the military, the insurgents (i.e., the Farabundo Marti National Liberation Front—FMLN), and the United States—was ready for the aftermath of 50 years of authoritarian governance. Then, second, from the end of 1981 to the end of 1984, the Salvadoran revolutionaries seemed to unify and appeared to be well on their way to a military victory and the assumption of power in their own right. Clearly, the FMLN was ascendant. Third, by the end of 1984, however, the Salvadoran armed forces had taken the best the insurgents could give and were beginning to regain control of the military situation. The period 1985–1989 was a time of relative impasse and negotiations. Fourth, the resultant 1992 Accords finally gave the Salvadoran government the objectives that it had articulated as early as 1984. The accords also allowed demobilized revolutionaries to be assimilated into the liberal-democratic process. However, following the classic Marxist-Leninist strategy of talk-talk-fight-fight, the FMLN launched an ill-timed offensive in the midst of the ongoing negotiations, and lost much if not all credibility. After that, it was only a matter of a short period of time before the conventional insurgency ended.[15]

Findings

The primary objective of the FMLN was to take down the incumbent Salvadoran government and replace it with one that would see the insurgents "take power and make the profound changes needed in the Salvadoran society."[16] This was stated repeatedly over the course of the war. The FMLN strategy changed from time to time in recognition of changing political-military conditions, but the fundamental assumption remained.

The first insurgent strategy was implemented well before the Salvadoran government or the United States determined that a problem existed. This organizational effort was an attempt to develop cadres of future leaders, politicize and organize the "masses," and begin the unification of the various "democratic" elements in the country. The intent was to create a single revolutionary organization for the conduct of the struggle.[17] That objective was finally achieved in 1980 when Fidel Castro made it a condition for his support.[18]

The second strategy was directed toward the government. In late 1979, indirect and direct attacks were initiated, first against the regime of General Romero and then against the civil-military *junta* that replaced him. The indirect part of the strategy was a psychological campaign to discredit the regime in power and to claim the "right" to govern in the name of political, social, and economic justice.[19] The direct attack came in the form of a limited but "final" offensive that began in 1981. Buoyed by the guerrilla successes in Nicaragua and armed with more than 600 tons of weapons and ammunition from Cuba, the FMLN leadership attempted to override the preparatory tenets of Marxist-Leninist strategy and take immediate control of the government through Che Guevara's concept of the force of arms.[20] At the same time, the insurgent leadership overestimated the degree of popular support and underestimated the ability of the Salvadoran armed forces.[21] The result, of course, was failure and rationalization of the effort as the beginning of the "general" offensive that would achieve the final objective. That strategy remained in effect until mid-1984.

By the end of 1984, the FMLN leadership apparently agreed that a shift of the center of gravity had taken place. The shift was from the enemy military force to the source of Salvadoran military power and to the external support for the government's reform efforts. That was the political, economic, and military aid provided by the United States. That strategy, then, became one of taking a relatively low profile militarily, negotiating, and waiting for the time when the United States would lose interest in the conflict and go home.[22] As a consequence, the FMLN broke down into small units to continue assassinations, kidnappings, and general terrorism on a carefully measured scale designed to constantly harass and intimidate the population and the government. These tactics were aimed at lessening regime legitimacy in terms of the ability to govern and protect the citizenry. In this connection, the insurgents continued to attack transportation and communications networks and the general economic infrastructure in order to sabotage government attempts to do anything that might improve personal and collective stability. At the same time, these tactics were intended to impress upon the United States the futility of its economic and military aid to El Salvador.[23]

Outcome

The endgame of the Salvadoran insurgency began in 1989 with serious diminishing support from the Soviet Union and Cuba. This resulted in the beginning of serious negotiations between the Salvadoran government and the FMLN. At the same time, support for the Salvadoran government from the United States was not what it might have been. As an example, this problem was highlighted by the unwillingness or inability of senior policy makers in Washington, DC, to develop any kind of coordinated effort to deal with the situation, despite the general willingness and commitment of both the Carter and Reagan administrations to help. A perceived "too little too late" conundrum during this crucial period illustrates the issue. Dr. Alvaro Magana, who acted as the Salvadoran president during the 1982–1984 period, argued that there appeared to have been no agreed-on, coherent strategy to achieve objectives and, indeed, no agreement as to what those objectives ought to be. Decisions concerning the allocation of "North American" resources to El Salvador appeared to have been made on the basis of what the minimum effort might be that could be made while maintaining congressional support for administration policy. As a matter of fact, the only alternative policies examined involved different force levels for the Salvadoran army and specific amounts of economic and military aid. Thus, issues addressed and decisions made were always tactical and short term in nature—that is, the typical bureaucratic "in-box drill" of finding a "quick fix," selling it, and getting rid of the immediate problem.[24]

Even so, with the disintegration of the Soviet Union and the withdrawal of support to the FMLN, it was only a matter of time before the insurgents would be completely unable to maintain their manpower and operations. Consequently, in 1992, a settlement was finally negotiated between the Salvadoran government and the FMLN, and the war was ended.

Conclusions

Four things stand out in strategic perspective. First, legitimacy was reaffirmed as the factor that in the long term would illustrate the absolute need to supplement military action with a rigorous application of a moral dimension to contemporary war. Second, the classic principles of unity of effort and a whole-of-government approach to conflict are reaffirmed as necessary for survival and perhaps even for moderate success. Third, external support to the insurgents made their efforts possible, and "North American" aid to the Salvadoran government probably saved that government. Fourth, at that critical point, the United States declared victory and went home.

KEY POINTS AND LESSONS

Key Points

- In the beginning of the El Salvadoran insurgency, the FMLN leadership adopted a model of guerrilla war made popular by Che Guevara.
- Guevara ignored the wisdom of Vladimir Ilyich Lenin regarding the conditions necessary to conduct a successful revolution. Guevara argued that an insurrection, in itself, would create the conditions necessary to generate radical political-economic-social change in given polity. Such an insurgency could be organized by a relatively small but mobile group of guerrilla fighters.
- During the period between 1985 and 1992, Salvadoran civil and military leaders and FMLN leadership began to understand that in addition to conventional insurgency there are additional wars within the war that must be acknowledged and mastered. Examples would include a war for relative perceived legitimacy, a war of information, a war to reduce external and internal support to the opponent, and a war of subversion.
- That there are viable alternatives to violent models for achieving fundamental change was validated.
- Strategies may be altered from time to time in recognition of changing political-military conditions.

Lessons

There are at least two extremely important lessons here. First, General John R. Galvin argues that if you draw a triangle and put the guerrillas at one corner, the government at the other corner, and the people at the third corner, then you have an equation (i.e., the "remarkable trinity"). The government must fight the guerrillas in such a way that it achieves the confidence of the people because, after all, that is what the guerrillas are really seeking. Both the guerrillas and the government are fighting to gain the support of the people. Every action that is taken must have that trinity at its base. That is the most important lesson to be learned. Now, to move to the military, the lesson is that the military must fight the war in such a way that it maintains the confidence of the people. That means it must be correct ethically and morally and, of course, professionally. It is not good enough just to be good guys. You have to know how to fight, too. There needs to be a balance of these elements. You have to be good solid fighters, and you have to be able to gain the confidence of the people. The people are the equation.[25]

Second, Ambassador Edwin G. Corr points out that once a war is declared to be over, that may not, in fact, be the case. In reality, the postwar period is every bit as important as the war itself. In the Salvadoran case, once the war was declared to be over that country entered a crucial point in its history. Ambassador Corr understood the situation correctly. His reasoning was prophetic. "I believe that if this stability stage is not exploited correctly in all its aspects—militarily, socially, and developmental—the insurgency could go back to a higher level of violence—or something even worse. If there is failure in any one of these areas, there will be failure sooner or later in all the others. If we can get the help to make external and internal conditions more favorable, the Salvadorans have the ability, the skills, the energy, and the entrepreneurial knowledge that would enable them to develop their beautiful country into an increasingly prosperous and safe place to live. What is needed from the United States is a bipartisan and prolonged commitment to stay as long as necessary to provide the guidance and other resources essential to make certain that democracy and peace are firmly established."[26]

As we all know, that did not happen. It deserves repeating that the United States declared victory and went home. Today, El Salvador is one of the poorest, most corrupt, and dangerous places in the world. On the other hand, Malaysia is doing relatively well.

CHAPTER 7

From Sovereignty Back to Security—or Not: Lessons from Venezuela (1998–Present) and Uruguay (1962–2005)

In terms of national security equating back to stability and well-being, it is helpful to review the linkage among security, stability, development, liberal democracy, responsible governance, and sustainable peace. This linkage involves the circular nature of the interdependent relationship among those elements that, in fact, define contemporary security. Importantly, the interdependent nature of these elements dictates that, if even only one of these defining elements is left out of this security equation, the result is virtually nothing. We also note that, to be effective, the circular nature of this equation requires the development of an upward—constructive—spiral. Otherwise, a static or negative, deconstructive, and downward process leads to a situation in which the state will be able to control less and less of its national territory and fewer and fewer of the people in it. That is a zero-sum game in which the state may dissolve, become a part of other states, and/or reconfigure into an entirely new entity. At the same time, much of the population might become refugees—or worse.

Venezuela provides contrasting positive and negative examples of this phenomenon. Consequently, this chapter will (1) review the peace-security paradigm and (2) move directly to the vignette. This vignette explores the entirety of the state failure threat. That threat is found in the opposite of the legitimate and competent state control of the national territory and the people in it. A second vignette examines a contrasting example of an insurgent program that slowly and bloodlessly took the Uruguayan Tupamaros from defeat to legitimate governance.

A REVIEW OF THE PEACE-SECURITY PARADIGM

Introduction and Context

The SWORD model (i.e., the peace-security model) takes into account the major unifying and legitimizing dimensions of the development of stability, a just civil society, and a sustainable peace. As a whole, this begins to define security, peace, and victory in the contemporary security environment. Additional steps toward those ends must be built on a foundation of carefully thought-out long-term, phased planning and implementation processes that are based on the seven dimensions of the SWORD model and the independent variables that define the crucial legitimacy variable. Three broadly inclusive elements contribute most directly to the allegiance of the populace and the achievement of a sustainable peace. They are establishing stability, regenerating and bolstering economic prosperity, and nurturing legitimate governance that would take us back to an enhanced level of security (i.e., sovereignty), again and again.[1]

First, as noted again and again, security begins with the provision of personal and collective stability. Providing stability to the individual members of a society is probably the most critical societal requirement. It requires a unified whole-of-government approach and is the primary basis on which popular allegiance to the state is built. Stability includes establishing law and order and the rule of law as a part of ensuring collective and personal well-being. Stability also includes the isolation of violent political and criminal factions from all sources of internal and external support. That leads to sustaining life, relieving suffering, and beginning the regeneration of the economy.

Second, as noted earlier, security and stability require regenerating the economy. That requires providing meaningful work and pay to individuals. This need not, and probably cannot, lead to immediate prosperity, but if it obviously leads to a reasonable hope for things to steadily improve—especially for one's children—it will prove to be adequate to the task at hand. That provides another sense of personal security and gives people hope for a meaningful future. On the other hand, if a people have no stake in the society and no hope for the future, their usual option is to resort to violence to force some kind of radical change.

Third, the need to provide for the socioeconomic development of a people is generally well understood. But, socioeconomic development is clearly not sufficient to generate long-term stability. That requires political competence and moral rectitude. To generate a viable political competence that can and will manage, coordinate, and sustain socioeconomic-political stability, two additional objectives must be achieved. First, a regime must foster popular political consent. Then, the regime must establish and maintain peaceful societal conflict-resolution processes. With these additional building blocks in place, a legitimate civil society becomes a real possibility. Lastly, to create a sustainable civil society, responsible sovereignty, and a durable internal peace, a legitimate government must deal effectively with the root causes of an internal conflict. Otherwise, governments will face growing socioeconomic-political unrest, criminal anarchy, possible state failure, overthrow, and the aftermath of state failure.

Fourth, the linkage among security, stability, development, liberal democracy, responsible sovereignty, and back again to sovereignty, that is, stability clearly is circular. Again, as noted earlier, maintenance of the status quo ante is not adequate to the task of generating and maintaining responsible sovereignty and a sustainable peace. To be really effective, the circular nature of this paradigm requires the development of an upward—constructive— spiral. Finding solutions to this set of issues takes the international community or other individual intervening actors beyond providing some form of humanitarian assistance in cases of human misery and need. It takes international political powers beyond traditional monitoring of bilateral agreements or protecting a people from another group of people or a government. It takes nation-states and international organizations beyond compelling one or another party to a conflict to cease human rights abuses and other morally repugnant practices. It also takes nation-states and international organizations beyond repelling some form of conventional military aggression.

Fifth, in these terms, stability requires more than a traditional tactical-level military-police (i.e., law enforcement) effort to become involved in a given conflict, establish a certain degree of physical security, and "declare victory and go home" or back to the barracks. The reality of such irresponsibility is that the destructive consequences of malgovernance are left to smolder and reignite at a later date with the accompanying human and monetary costs. So, how can all this be sorted out? Nobody knows for certain. What we can assume with any degree of certainty, however, is that the consequences of declaring victory and going home, or back to the barracks, result in a "continuing struggle without clemency that exacts the highest political tension."[2]

To help those with the responsibility of dealing with contemporary conflict at any given level, the SWORD peace-security paradigm provides a conceptual framework that aids decision makers, policy makers, and implementers in pointing out what they need to know about contemporary security problems. It also aids them in choosing ways and means to achieve their geostrategic ends. However, it is no panacea and does not relieve policy makers and decision makers from cognitive preparation and tough decisions. It essentially provides the necessary overarching framework within which decision makers and policy makers can study, question, make decisions, and act. The intent is to establish the conditions that will lead to the strategic geopolitical objective of a better, more just, and more secure world—one part at a time.[3] As noted earlier, Venezuela provides a negative example of this phenomenon.

VIGNETTE 1: VENEZUELA FROM SOVEREIGNTY BACK TO SECURITY—OR NOT

Background

Caudillos (strong men)—including "The Liberator" Simon Bolivar—dominated Venezuela in a succession of military dictatorships from independence in 1821 to the coup against the dictatorship of President Marcos Perez Jimenez and the subsequent military *junta* in 1958. During that 137-year period, more than 20 constitutions were drafted, promulgated, and ignored. More than 50 armed revolts took their toll of life and property. Political parties meant little and political principles even less. In all, Venezuela exhibited the characteristics of a traditional authoritarian society until the oil industry began to boom after World War II.

The modern political forces set in motion by a robust oil economy produced an experiment in democracy that was tempered by a strong central government. That government included a corporatist executive authority and security apparatus organized to direct and control the political and economic life of the country. That government was built upon a pact among members of the elites under which the dominant political parties and their "caudilloistic" leaders were the principal actors. As Maximilien Robespierre did after the French Revolution, Venezuelan leaders determined what they believed was best for themselves and then for all citizens. That became the general will. Thus, the Venezuelan state controlled the wealth produced by its petroleum and other industries and was the principal distributor of the surpluses generated by a highly regulated and subsidized economy. To one extent or another—and some more than others—all the people and every enterprise in Venezuela feed off what has been called the *piñata* (a suspended breakable pot filled with candies for children's parties) of the state treasury.[4]

In these conditions, ambitious political leaders have found it easy to exploit popular grievances to catapult themselves into power—and try to stay there. As a consequence, through mass mobilization, supporting demonstrations, and subtle and not-so-subtle coercion, demagogic populist leaders are in a position to claim a mandate to place themselves above elections, political parties, legislatures, and courts and to govern as they see fit. Somehow, citizens and outside observers have expected these "democratically elected" governments to move Venezuela to stability, economic development, civil peace, and individual prosperity. Instead, those governments stagnate. They remain as closed as ever. Meaningful development fails to take place. Political turmoil and violence prevail. Ordinary people continue to live in relative poverty, and caudilloistic populists reinforce their radical positions by inflaming anti-U.S. sentiment.[5]

Findings: Hugo Chavez's Bolivarian Vision and How to Achieve It

Hugo Chavez's abbreviated geopolitical end state was to develop the potential of Latin America to achieve Simon Bolivar's dream of Lain American political-economic integration and *grandeza* (i.e., magnificence), to reduce the U.S. hegemony in the region, and to change the geopolitical map of the Western Hemisphere.[6] The idea was that sooner or later a socialistic Bolivarian political-economic system would extend throughout all of the Americas. The movement toward achieving that geopolitical objective would begin with the premise that traditional post–World War II socialist and Marxist-Leninist political-economic models made mistakes, but the theory remains valid.[7]

Chavez's strategic-level dream depends on five operational-level concepts. The idea here is that representative democracy and the U.S.-dominated capitalism of the new global era are total failures. These failures must be replaced by "direct democracy" and a socialist economy. Thus, Chavez adopted (1) the Rousseauian concept of "direct" or "totalitarian" democracy and (2) a socialist economic system as two parts of a five-part overarching political-economic model for Venezuela and the rest of the Latin America. The other three parts of the model included (1) social programs to strengthen "direct democracy," (2) maximum communications support to the regime, and (3) a new security scheme for Venezuela that would ensure internal peace and social harmony in the country. That security scheme would also provide the foundations for a Hemisphere-wide regional power bloc and eventual socioeconomic and political integration.[8]

The Political and Economic Concepts

As noted earlier, Venezuelan democracy has its roots firmly in the French Revolution and the subsequent perversions of the Rousseauian notion of "total" or "direct" (i.e., totalitarian) democracy. In these terms, the individual citizen surrenders his or her rights and personal interests to the state in return for the enforcement of social harmony and the general will. Thus, the state enjoys absolute power (i.e., de facto sovereignty) through the enforcement of the general will. The main tenets of Venezuelan democracy dictate that the authority in the state must be a maximum leader who communicates directly with the people, interprets their needs, and emphasizes "social expenditure" to guarantee the legitimate needs and desires of the people. Elections, congress, and the courts will provide formal democracy and international acceptance (i.e., de jure sovereignty) but will have no real role in governance or the economy. The state will control or own the major means of production and distribution. As a consequence, the national and regional political-socioeconomic integration and development functions will be performed by the maximum leader by means of his or her "total" authority.[9]

The Social Programs and Communications Concepts

To strengthen his personal position and internal power base, Chavez intended to spend large amounts of money on an amorphous Plan Bolivar 2000 for building and renovation of schools, clinics, day nurseries, roads, and housing for the poor. Additionally, the maximum leader wanted to develop education and literacy outreach programs, agrarian reform programs, and workers' cooperatives. He established Mercal, a state-owned company that was intended to provide subsidized foodstuffs to the poor. Chavez also imported 16,000 Cuban doctors to help take care of the medical needs of the Venezuelan underclass. Clearly, these social programs would offer tangible benefits to the mass of voting Venezuelans who had been generally ignored or neglected by previous governments. Unfortunately, however, many of these well-intended programs never came into being or were not able to fulfill their legitimizing functions.[10]

The intent of these communications and informational efforts was to generate strong and favorable public opinion. *Bolivarianismo* requires maximum media support to purvey ideas, develop mass consensus, and generate political successes. Ample evidence exist that Chavez-controlled media were using emotional arguments to gain attention, exploit real and imagined fears, create outside enemies as scapegoats for internal failures, and inculcate the notion that opposition to the regime equates to betrayal of the country. Chavez's personal involvement in the communications effort was also clear and strong. His statements, speeches, and interviews have been broadcast throughout Venezuela, the Caribbean Basin, and large parts of Central and South America every day on the state-owned *Television del Sur*.[11]

The Security Scheme

The Venezuelan Constitution of 1999 provided political and institutional autonomy for the armed forces, under the absolute control of the president and the commander in chief. President Chavez also created an independent national police force outside the traditional control of the armed forces, which is directly responsible to the president. At the same time, the president set in motion the establishment of a 1-million-person military reserve and two additional paramilitary organizations—the *Frente Bolivariano de Liberacion* (Bolivarian Liberation Front) and the *Ejercito del Pueblo en Armas* (Army of the People in Arms). The armed forces and the police perform traditional national defense and internal security missions within the context of preparing for what President Chavez called a fourth-generation asymmetric "war of all the people." The military reserve and the paramilitary (militia) organizations were charged to protect the country from a U.S. or Colombian invasion with an internal *jihadist*-type insurgency and to act internationally as armed antibourgeois militias. The institutional separation of the various security organizations ensures that no one security institution can control the others. The centralization of those institutions under the control of the president, however, would ensure his absolute control of security and social harmony in Venezuela.[12]

More Findings

Additionally, still thinking at the operational level, President Chavez knew that asymmetric conflict is a logical and powerful means of expression and self-assertion. It is a concept as old as war itself. It is a methodology of the weak against the strong. He also knew that asymmetric conflict is not won by seizing specific territory militarily or destroying specific industrial or nuclear capabilities. It is won by altering the political-psychological-economic-social factors that are most relevant in a targeted culture. As a result, in 2004, Chavez, along with Fidel Castro and Raul Castro, created the Bolivarian Alliance of the Americas (ALBA). It now consists of 13 countries in Latin America and the Caribbean Basin and has its own trading organization, bank, and TV network. The stated intent of the alliance is to conduct a negative narrative against the U.S. imperialism in the Western Hemisphere and to do as much as possible to generate public discord in the area. In these terms, it is important to note that ALBA has been known to provide material and political support to various insurgent and drug trafficking organizations in the Hemisphere.[13]

Lastly, Chavez's ambitious operational-level thinking also included a three-front asymmetric war of all the people that (1) is psychological-political, (2) uses combinations of asymmetric ways and means to achieve its ends, and (3) is deliberately protracted.[14]

All this was not the thinking or rhetoric of a "nut case," a "clown," or even a man immersed in "political theater." Lt. Colonel Chaves was a dedicated revolutionary and an astute warrior who understood asymmetric war. He knew that his revolutionary vision would not be achieved through a conventional military war of maneuver and attrition or a "Che" Guevara-type insurgency. Rather, a "new (utopian) society" would be created by exporting instability and generating public opinion in favor of the "revolution" and against the U.S.-controlled bourgeois system. The geostrategic objectives of that long-term effort would be achieved only by a gradual and systematic Leninist application of agitation and propaganda.[15] The reality of this revolutionary thinking is that instead of providing stability, developing socioeconomic-political development, and creating competent political leadership, Chavez chose to "destroy in order to build." That reality extends to the fact that just as the world has evolved from an industrial society to an information-based society, so has warfare. The primary instruments of warfare are now agitation and propaganda. The one thing that remains the same is that, at one level or another, compulsion of any kind still defines war. Consequently, it also defines stability and security—and instability and insecurity.

Outcome

As noted earlier, when Chavez died, he did not leave behind a politically and morally competent cadre capable of developing and enhancing domestic stability at home and, at the same time, conducting a successful asymmetric Bolivarian war abroad. It did not help when oil prices dropped sharply, leaving the regime without the monetary resources necessary to keep the *piñata* full and the plutocrats and the citizens happy. As a consequence, Venezuela is basically what it always has been—only much worse under Maduro. The country continues to be governed by a plutocratic class dependent on oil, but the *piñata* is almost empty. The majority of the people are being fooled and remain as excluded as ever.[16] Under President Maduro's leadership, Venezuela has moved into a downward spiral from an aspiring new socialist state to a failing state status.

Now, interestingly and importantly, it is within the realm of possibility that the downward trajectory of Chavez's "Plan A" would take Venezuela down the way toward a "Plan B," that is, a dictatorship of the proletariat, also known as democratic centralism. This might be what he intended all along. It might well be that a Venezuelan state failure would destroy all vestiges of liberal democracy and capitalism. With that, the country's socialist leadership could take control of the means of production, distribution, communication, socioeconomic programs, and the state security apparatus. In turn, it would be relatively easy to build a model of a new socialist republic. Some savants argue that efforts directed at controlling unconventional communications and social program centers of gravity are merely political theater. They are absolutely right. What they do not understand, however, is that empirical data strongly indicate that this political theater is extremely effective in generating radical political, economic, and social change. This transition is geostrategic and epochal in scale. It justifies democratic centralism and resultant coercive political culture that can take a polity from the demonstrated misery of liberal democracy and capitalism to the promised love and harmony of new socialism.

The Resultant Implosion

In any event, at least five indicators identify that downward trajectory. They are as follows: (1) a weakening economy, unemployment, starvation, inflation, and major refugee flow. As examples, *Latinometro* and journalistic data tell us that economic progress and unemployment are the principal problems plaguing Latin America; (2) that data also tell us that Venezuela ranks second out of 18 Latin American countries in which the economy and unemployment are the most important problems in the country. Ecuador ranked first; (3) 58 percent of the Venezuelan population declared that they do not have sufficient food to live on. Reportedly, 30 percent of the people eat only once a day. This is the highest percentage in all of the Latin American countries; (4) inflation in Venezuela is also the highest in Latin America. The figures are astronomical and go up every day, leaving the rest of Latin America and the world way behind; (5) lastly, and again, Venezuela ranks first in Latin America in terms of refugee flow. Well over 4 million Venezuelans have left the country since Chavez rose to power. As only one example, since the beginning of 2018, more than 55,000 Venezuelans are reported to have moved to Ecuador. At the same time, more than 4,000 Venezuelans are reported to be entering that impoverished country every day. Brazil, Colombia, and Peru are also having to deal with the same problems every day.[17]

Conclusions

Political theater is extremely effective in creating political-economic-social disequilibrium, weakening an adversary, and generating radical political-economic-social change. It is a proven means through which to create stability, strengthen a given political-economic-social system, and develop the political culture that can take a polity to a sustainable peace and security (i.e., sovereignty).

The same people who argue that emphasizing the "new" strategic-level communications and social program centers of gravity as political theater also argue that Lt. Colonel Chavez was a clown. Not so. He was a warrior who knew what he was doing. He knew that he would be the last man standing—no matter how badly beaten up he might be—who is the winner in contemporary asymmetric conflict. As a consequence, there might well have been a "Plan C." If history is any indicator, the last man standing might be someone in uniform—or someone supported by someone in uniform—who understands the concept of asymmetric Bolivarian war.

Lessons: A Cautionary Tale

The contemporary security dialogue is beginning to focus on enhancing popular perceptions of relative stability and well-being. This tends to refer to the use of a variety of means—only one of which is military—in the circular and upward pursuit of national stability, well-being, effective sovereignty, security, peace, and then to a higher level of stability. In these terms, the enemy can be the state or nonstate actor who plans and implements the kind of kinetic and/or nonkinetic coercion that threatens any aspect of the security cycle and exploits the root causes of instability. In this context, three issues must be addressed.

First, various nonstate actors and some state actors—who are not supposed to be anything but bit players in the global security arena—are creating a Hobbesian anarchy in which life is nasty, brutish, and short. If left ignored and unchecked, this unconventional and asymmetric chaos facilitates an epochal transition from the traditional Westphalian nation-state system and Western liberal democratic values to unwanted alternative governance and values. This Hobbesian anarchy also facilitates a tidal wave of globally destabilizing migrants, refugees, internally displaced individuals, and slaves.

Second, in responding to the utopian dreams and destabilizing activities of contemporary belligerent state and nonstate actors, Albert Camus admonishes us to understand that those who dream of epochal change "... have turned their backs upon the fixed radiant point of the present. They forget the present for the future, the fate of humanity for the delusion of power, the misery of the slums for the mirage of the eternal city, ordinary justice for an empty promised land. They despair of personal freedom and dream of a strange freedom of the species; reject solitary death and give the name of mortality to a vast collective agony. ... [They] entertain the puerile belief that to love one single day of life amounts to justifying whole centuries of oppression. ... For want of something better to do, they deify themselves."[18]

Third, the consequences of failing to take this strategic political-psychological effort seriously are clear. Unless thinking, action, and organization are oriented at the highest levels to deal with asymmetric knowledge-based information and technology realities, the problems of global, regional, and subregional stability and security will resolve themselves—and not likely for the better.

VIGNETTE 2: FROM DEFEAT TO LEGITIMATE GOVERNANCE IN FOUR STAGES—URUGUAY (1962–2005)

Introduction

Uruguay in one of the few counties in the world that has a long history of experience in representative democracy, peaceful stability, and inclusive processes. That political culture gives Uruguay advantages and possibilities for political-economic-social development that are not trivial or well understood outside the country. As a consequence, three cultural realities are critical to understanding the Tupamaro insurgency (i.e., National Liberation Movement [MLN]), 1962–2005. First, if anything politically serious happens, it takes place slowly. Second, Uruguayan political-economic-social tradition will exert a strong influence. Third, Uruguayans, over time, will transform a cultural problem into a nonproblem. Given these cultural realities, one can see how and why the MLN and the Uruguayan civilian and military leadership achieved their strategic objectives—that is, one can see how and why the military defeat of the MLN and long years of repression, rethinking, and reorganization eventually came together peacefully and democratically.

Context

Uruguay was and still is a small country of approximately 3.5 million inhabitants. Most of the population are of European stock and 70–80 percent live in or near the capital city of Montevideo. The interior of the country is very thinly populated and has been developed into large sheep and cattle ranches and other agricultural enterprises. The socioeconomic pattern was developed in the last quarter of the nineteenth century when a large influx of Spanish and Italian emigrants arrived in the country. That boosted the nation's workforce and also expanded the strong middle-class section of the population. Between 1903 and 1915, the government was in the hands of men of considerable political skill and reforming zeal, and it was at this time that the bases for the country's political freedom were consolidated.[19]

In the 1960s and 1970s, the economic development and almost universal prosperity came to an end. The precipitous decline in living standards incited public demands for economic and governmental reforms. The problem was that, by the early 1960s, the Uruguayan government comprised a constitutionally determined number of elected officials and an unconstrained number of appointed or hired bureaucrats. The number of bureaucrats was estimated to be equivalent to 20 percent of the entire Uruguayan population.[20] The declining economy was unable to sustain such an unbalanced drain on public finances. Moreover, that bloated bureaucracy was never credited with paying much attention to the needs of the state or society. The government, at best, had become a personal enrichment process. At its worst, some individuals held two or three government jobs at the same time. There was no accountability, depending on one's relationship with a given chief or section. Those unmonitored jobs in the bureaucracy would allow an employee to come and go at will and to collect two or three relatively lucrative government salaries at the same time. After a few years, one could *jubilarse temrano* (retire early) and live a quite comfortable life.[21]

As a result, members of the "political class"—along with their brothers and sisters-in-law, cousins, and other retainers—were unwilling to give up the easy lifestyle and a secure future. The motive, simply, was greed. Consequently, by the mid-1960s, the government and its bureaucracy had mobilized the legal-constitutional and political-military institutions and resources of the state for their own purposes. That could be seen in government's inability and/or unwillingness to maintain decent roads, education, health, and other public services for most of the Uruguayan society. That could also be seen in governmental repression, the creation of a military-controlled dictatorship, serious popular unrest, and the motivation from which the Tupamaro insurgency developed.

Findings 1: The Process of State Failure and Eventual Regeneration

That destabilizing situation took the country into a downward spiral of instability, social violence, political-economic degradation, and insecurity. Additionally and importantly, that downward spiral took Uruguay into a failing state status. The failing state status took the country from democracy to insurgency and dictatorship. Then, the Uruguayan political tradition took the country back to democracy again.[22] Ironically, over time, the Uruguayan political tradition and strong popular support invalidated the Tupamaro program.

The major premise around which Uruguay's inclusive political tradition was constructed is the recognition of the fundamental freedom of an individual. It comes from a deep and abiding faith in human reason. Thus, every belief or every opinion has the right to be stated and published without hindrance, and the intelligence of the individual is sufficient to distinguish truth from error and to treat harmful or antisocial ideas as they deserve. Moreover, every school child in the country was taught that the government of a free country respects the rights of the groups as well as individuals. The two types of rights are not completely separate from one another. Rather, the rights of speech, association, political choice, and other individual freedoms are associated with responsible democratic governance. Uruguay's distinctive political culture further required a combination of intellectual honesty and willingness to compromise. This political culture was well enough engrained in the Uruguayan population to enable it to survive insurgency war and the subsequent military dictatorship.[23]

The process of state failure and eventual rejuvenation takes us back to a more detailed examination of the contextual realities of Uruguayan politics. The overall timeline goes like the following:

1966: A new constitution voided the old *colegiado* (i.e., collegiate) executive department of government and provided for a single president. The council comprised six members. Four seats went to the majority party and two seats were reserved for the minority party.

1967: President Pacheco Areco unilaterally banned six leftist newspapers.

1968: The president decreed a state of emergency in which most civil and human rights were curtailed.

1970: The president initiated a newspaper censorship process and closed those papers that would not accept censorship.

1972: The president made a Declaration of Internal War and gave the armed forces *carta blanca* (a free hand) to deal with the Tupamaros (i.e., the MLN).

1972: The armed forces began to replace the national police in dealing with the MLN.

1973: All left-wing political activities were eliminated, and the MLN was defeated.

1973–1982: All political parties and activities were banned. The national university was closed. All workers' organizations were outlawed. Repression, jailing, killing, and torture continued without constraint.

The late 1960s and 1970s: The economic development and almost universal prosperity came to an end. Public demands for economic and political reforms generated a succession of polls, elections, plebiscites, and mass rallies that over time demonstrated the political resolve of the Uruguayan people. The Uruguayan political tradition, then, exerted itself and the people began to fight back the only way they could—with their votes and support of polls, plebiscites, and mass rallies. People were arrested, jailed, tortured, and killed, but the "people" eventually prevailed.

1983: In mid-1983, the military government increased levels of repression and press censorship. The result was a series of mass demonstrations demanding an immediate return to democracy.

1985: Free and fair elections were held. A civilian government under President Julio Maria Sanguinetti reinstated civilian governance. The new government promulgated a blanket amnesty, pardoned MLN leadership, and allowed the Tupamaros to reemerge as a legitimate political party.

2005: The Tupamaro candidate, Tabare Vazquez, was elected President of the Republic.

2005–Present: Uruguay and the rest of the world witnessed the return to responsible governance, an acceptable level of economic development, and sustainable peace (i.e., security).[24]

Findings 2: The Emergence and Demise of the Tupamaro National Liberation Movement

The internal conflict situation in Uruguay between 1962 and 1973 was relatively straightforward. The government had failed to maintain the economic and political underpinnings of peace and prosperity. Insurgency, terrorism, and their associated asymmetry emerged in the form of the Tupamaro MLN in direct response to that organization's perception of political, economic, and social injustice.

The first step in the formation of the MLN was taken in 1961 by Raul Sendic. He was a 35-year-old law student from Montevideo who had led a group of sugar farmers from the Paysandu area in a protest against low pay and poor working conditions. After a term in prison for his role in that public demonstration, Sendic and a group of his friends moved back to the capital city of Montevideo. They rightly considered Montevideo's urban setting to be a much more suitable base location for guerrilla warfare than Uruguay's sparsely populated interior. Quite simply, there are no possibilities for mountain or jungle sanctuaries in that habitat.

Sendic's Tupamaros, however, did not rush into military action. It was not until December 1966 that they confronted police in an armed action, and it was not until 1968 that they publicly announced their political objective of deposing the Uruguayan government. In the meantime, this group of about 20 individuals cultivated a "Robin Hood" image by conducting a series of bank robberies and seizures of money and food that were distributed to the poor. As a result, a poll in 1971 showed that 59 percent of the Uruguayan people thought the Tupamaros to be an organization motivated by social justice and altruistic motives.[25] That kind of effort was considered worthwhile, challenging, and even fun. It was good to be a Tupamaro at that time.

The purpose of this altruism was to "generate conscience, organization, and the conditions for the revolution,"[26] even though nobody seemed to know what that might involve. Nobody seemed to be greatly concerned because everybody expected that taking down the government and creating a nationalistic, socialistic, and popular democracy would resolve everything. There was a problem here, however. There seems to have been no vision of what a nationalistic, socialistic, and popular democracy might be. The motive of the Tupamaros became the revolution for revolution's sake. With the long-term political aims of the insurgency beginning to become more and more ambiguous, the Tupamaros became more and more arrogant and militaristic. Robberies and kidnappings increased. Killings and confrontations with police and the military also increased. Taxes on the well-to-do middle class and businesses were increased. Jailbreaks were planned and implemented. Money that had gone to provide for the poor went to the purchase of businesses and weapons. Attacks on military targets became more and more sophisticated and frequent. The MLN also created "people's prisons" in which they interrogated, held, and executed their own prisoners. In all, the populace perceived the Tupamaros to be running a parallel government and parallel system of repression. Others perceived the Tupamaros to be closer to resembling a parallel power—something like the mafia. In any event, the MLN was not considered to be anything like a liberating movement of the masses.[27] Consequently, as a result of losing sight of its original political objectives and the loss of popular support, the Tupamaros began to suffer severe reversals that ended with their complete defeat in 1972–1973.

Outcome

The outcome of the actions of the Tupamaros, the government, and the Uruguayan people between 1962 and 1972 and then from 1972 through 2005 resulted in a series of four stages of obstacles and lessons. These lessons focused on the course of action chosen by a small minority group of "heretical" MLN leaders that took place after their surprisingly quick military defeat at the hands of the Uruguayan armed forces in April 1972. It was a hard decision to make, but it was the only way to survive and to continue the revolutionary struggle—that is, there were only two paths for the Tupamaros. The first was to adapt their revolutionary socialist program to the Uruguayan reality and live. The other was to continue fighting against reality and die. As a consequence, instead of continuing to replicate the recent Argentine (*Montonero*) insurgency and the resultant "Dirty War," a change in direction was required. These heretical and traitorous *tendencia nuevo tiempo* (modern-age tendency) MLN leaders knew that they had to go back, bypass "Che" Guevara's *foco* "military shortcut" to victory, and do what Lenin had recommended many years earlier—that is, Tupamaro leadership had to rethink the problem and go back to Leninist basics.

The results of that analysis were straightforward and cogent. First, the traditional Leninist conditions for revolution were not in place. The political, socioeconomic-psychological, and military "correlation of forces" had not been prepared, and the Uruguayan people were not convinced that exchanging the contemporary government dictatorship for a dictatorship of the "vanguard of the proletariat" would bring any great improvement. Second, the revolution and the new socialism of the contemporary period are no longer based on the clash of different parts of society (i.e., bourgeoisie versus proletariat). Rather, the new challenge that the revolution had to confront was the issue of responsible legitimate governance. This would not be a short-term effort and glorious entry into the offices of government such as that which Fidel Castro had carried out in Cuba in 1959. Instead, it would be a delicate, difficult, and long-term effort in which the Tupamaros would have to give the Uruguayan people the security, stability, and socioeconomic well-being that politicians of all colors had been promising forever.

The actions required to initiate the first stage and related obstacle and lesson that led toward revolutionary success would generate a sea change in outlook and behavior. That first step was to separate from the main MLN group (i.e., *tendencia proletaria*: "proletarian tendency"), reject violent revolution, and pursue a peaceful democratic approach to fundamental change. That decision would take the minority MLN faction through three more stages of obstacles and lessons. Once the decision was made to pursue a peaceful solution to the problem, they had to overcome their inflammatory leftist rhetoric and transform their primary political objective from violent revolution to legitimate governance. Second, they had to overcome over a decade of isolation from the rest of the Uruguayan society and organize a coalition of other political parties that could eventually win free and fair elections. To do so, they required the development of a long-forgotten attitude of tolerance toward society and other parties—and the people in general. Third, and perhaps the most difficult, the "new" Tupamaros had to revise their long-held ideological concept of a rational political-economic system—that is, the "new" Tupamaros had to overcome the theoretical contradiction between capitalism and democracy. In these terms, they had to accept the reality of a European type of mixed economy. That required the acceptance of pluralist democracy and the rejection of democratic centralism (i.e., the dictatorship of the vanguard of the proletariat). In all, that change of the Tupamaros to "something they were not" took over 30 years to accomplish. But, accomplish it, they did. In the elections of 2005, the Tupamaro candidate was elected President of the Republic.

Conclusions

Lessons from over a half century of bitter experience suffered by governments, military institutions, insurgents, and other violent state and nonstate actors involved in various destabilizing and bloody internal conflicts show that a given response to a given threat often ends—or continues on and on—in greater violence and misery than ever anticipated. Too often, this is because too much time, treasure, and blood are dedicated to relatively ineffectual, tactical, and operational military efforts as opposed to defining and implementing a geostrategic endgame. The experience of the Tupamaro *tendencia proletaria* is a case in point. The Tupamaros' revolutionary tutor Abraham Guillen was blunt. He reminded his pupils that reliance on armed encounters and military action is a "procedure for piling up cadavers, for giving easy victories to repressive leaders."

As a result, the *tendencia nuevo tiempo* developed a carefully organized, holistic, and patiently implemented end-state plan. That organizing paradigm became the foundation for developing subordinate or more-specific plans that would make direct contributions to the mutually desired end state. The cornerstones of that foundation included legitimate governance, unity of effort, intelligence collection, and dissemination of information. All that would ensure a close, circular linkage among security, stability, socioeconomic development, societal peace, prosperity, and political freedom.[28] That end state came to fruition in 2005 with the election of a Tupamaro president of the Republic.

KEY POINTS AND LESSONS

Key Points

- Insurgent organizations tend to mobilize when internal economic and political turmoil reach crisis proportions. In the Uruguayan case, the incompetent and repressive response of the corrupt incumbent regime provided the final motivation from which the Tupamaro insurgency developed.

- Regular military forces can—with the application of enough power and little restraint—quickly defeat an irregular insurgent enemy.

- Military defeat of an insurgent organization does not resolve the root-cause problems that brought on the insurgency in the first place. Thus, there are important political and socioeconomic aspects of the situation that must also be addressed. Otherwise, the prospects for a country and its people are bleak.

- The Tupamaros began their insurgency with good organization and tactics and a positive relationship with the Uruguayan people. Over time, however, they lost sight of their political aims and strategy and also lost the support of the people. The Uruguayan case is a prime example of public opinion acting as a primary center of gravity in an internal conflict.

- Tupamaro recuperation and renewal and ultimate political success came as a result of the following four stages of obstacles and lessons that, once applied, exerted positive effects on public opinion: (1) they had to transform their primary political objectives from violent revolution to peaceful democratic change, (2) they had to reject the idea of the dictatorship of the vanguard of the proletariat and accept the concept of popular-based legitimate governance, (3) they had to overcome an intolerant exclusive political environment and create a tolerant inclusive political climate to win free and fair elections, and (4) they had to repudiate the concept that government ownership and control of the means of production and distribution was the only rational model for the national economy. Accordingly, they had to accede to the reality of a European model of a mixed economy that incorporated both capitalist and socialist features.

- Clearly, despite some understandable reluctance, modern-age Tupamaros realized that to become a movement that represents the masses and can get things done peacefully, they would need to formulate a program stressing that whatever unites the "forces of liberation" must be accomplished.

Lessons

The entire Tupamaro experience illustrates that there is a far superior alternative to violent and totalitarian models for fundamental political-economic-social change. Violent revolutionary models can depose governments, but they do not have a good record in dealing with the horrible aftermath of violent revolution nor are they known for their record in dealing with the root causes of revolution.

It would be a terrible thing to assume that there is nothing to be learned from the Tupamaro experience in Uruguay. That experience cannot be dismissed as an aberration or luck. It cannot be dismissed as taking too long, being too difficult, being too expensive, or being too idealistic. That attitude has proven to lead to horrific humanitarian disasters and a continually violent world. Thomas Hobbes would remind us again that that is a world in which life is nasty, brutish, and short.

Uruguay's own Jose Enrique Rodo teaches us that "The central feature of the situation . . . is that national and international leadership must not shirk the work of re-educating itself, of remolding itself." He argued that one should not wait for failure to begin a renewal process. Rather, renewal is a lifelong effort directed at attaining "real liberty." This applies to the individual as well as the state. "Nations that enjoy liberty change their thought, their tasks, and their goals—they struggle with their past to get away from it and improve themselves and the world." This is the baseline formula for "turning something that was, into something that it could and should be."[29] And, finally, the experience of the Uruguayan Tupamaros and the Venezuelan *Chavistas* illustrates the critical importance of the political competence component of the SWORD peace-security paradigm. Remember, $100 \times 0 = 0$.

CHAPTER 8

Toward a Paradigm for Foreign Policy and Power Asset Management—or Not: The Proxy War against the Soviet 40th Army in Afghanistan (1979–1989)

The strategic-level commonalities discussed in previous chapters would not have come as any kind of surprise to Sun Tzu, Machiavelli, Vladimir Ilyich Lenin, or Mao Tse-Tung. Nor would these common lessons come as news to a contemporary populist, neo-populist, new socialist, criminal nonstate actor, popular militia, or proxy. In these terms, the case study methodology that serves as the foundation for this book indicates that there are several long-standing political-strategic rules that when developed and integrated into a legitimizing and holistic conceptual scheme (i.e., paradigm) make the difference between winning and losing wars perpetrated by the contemporary politicized and violent nonstate actor phenomenon.

Five themes, or grand strategic guidelines, run through the various cases that inform this analysis. We find the following:

- Public opinion and political leadership is the "new" primary center of gravity.
- Legitimate governance is the "new" central strategic problem in contemporary security issues.
- Appropriate "smart" combinations of hard and soft power provide "new" ways to attack or counter an adversary.
- The key to putting all these elements together into a balanced strategic whole is an overarching theory of engagement (i.e., a paradigm) designed to deal specifically with a given conflict (i.e., war).

- Such a paradigm can be a major instrument of nation-state and/or nonstate power in attacking an adversary's strategy or in defending one's own.

It was not just a passing thought when Carl von Clausewitz stated that the public and the political leadership are the centers of gravity (i.e., the hub of all power and strength) in internal and external conflict. It was not just an incidental caution when Sun Tzu pointed out that legitimate (i.e., moral) governance, not just military capability, is the basis for success in war. It was not just a means of getting the attention of the prince when Machiavelli argued that good arms and good laws applied with *prudenza* (i.e., prudence) generate ultimate success in conflict. And, back to Clausewitz, he was not just being eloquent when he explained that the three elements of his "remarkable trinity" (i.e., the government, the military, and the people) must be brought into equilibrium with a unifying paradigm.

This brings us back to where we began and to the contemporary wisdom of Qiao Liang and Wang Xiangsui. They observe that we must come to terms with the fact that contemporary security, at whatever level, is at base a unified, holistic, multidimensional effort. They unequivocally argue that, regardless of when and where a conflict has taken place, the empirical data indicate that all victories or failures display two common qualities. They are as follows: the winner is the state or nonstate political actor who is best organized and disciplined. Additionally, the winner developed and implemented a unifying conceptual paradigm to guide the implementation of a classic long-term geopolitical end-state strategy.

Consequently, this chapter (1) reviews lessons learned over the past several years; (2) outlines the contemporary security dilemma; (3) sketches a paradigm for contemporary security policy; and (4) in addition to the conventional types of irregular intrastate conflicts already examined, we look at an excellent example of the depth, breadth, complexity, and effectiveness of proxy war—that is, the Afghan Mujahideen model for proxy war against the Soviet 40th Army, 1979–1989. Authoritatively, Bruce Riedel tells us that "for those who remember them, the lessons of the Afghan War will remain relevant and meaningful for years to come."[1]

REVIEW OF LESSONS LEARNED

The common denominator in our review of lessons learned is that, regardless of the degree of sophistication, hegemonic actors must eventually seize or control political power to guarantee the freedom of action and movement they need to achieve their various objectives. This requires control of the human terrain, not just the geographical terrain. In turn, this has created a dangerous synergy between organized criminality and terror that is blurring the traditional line between criminal and political violence. In the long term, the ultimate threat is state failure, the violent imposition of a radical socioeconomic-political restructuring of the nation-state and its governance, and the horrific aftermath of that radical change. The implications are clear and daunting.

What Violent, Politicized, Hegemonic "Bad Guys" Teach Us about Power

The rules that have governed conventional conflict are no longer completely valid. We must now struggle with a political reality that international law and convention are only beginning to address. The distinguished contemporary French political philosopher Jacques Maritain reminds us that the state is an instrument in the service of man—not the reverse. The highest functions of the State [are to] ensure the rule of law and facilitate the free development of the body politic. "Then, only will the State achieve its true dignity, which comes not from power and prestige, but from the exercise of justice."[2]

Consequently, power is no longer simply combat firepower directed against an enemy military formation or industrial capability. Power is now directed against entire populations. That requires a multidimensional political-economic social-psychological-informational-moral-military-police-civil bureaucratic activity that can be brought to bear appropriately on the causes as well as the perpetrators of violence. This may be achieved by those actors who understand Sun Tzu's "indirect approach"—that is, brain power, an understanding of diverse cultures, an appreciation of the power of dreams, and a mental flexibility that goes well beyond the traditional attrition war culture.[3]

The principal tools in this situation include the following: (1) intelligence operations; (2) public diplomacy at home and abroad; (3) information and propaganda operations; (4) cultural manipulation measures to influence and/or control public opinion and political decision-making leadership; and (5) foreign alliances, partnerships, and traditional diplomacy. There is no type of nonkinetic or kinetic power that cannot be mixed and matched with others. The only limitation would be one's imagination. That is why Qiao and Wang call contemporary violent politicized conflict "unrestricted war."[4]

Again, the reality of contemporary conflict is that information—not firepower—is the currency on which successful war is conducted. We must also remember that no regime, group, or force can legislate or decree moral legitimacy or political competence for themselves or anyone else. Legitimization, stability, and well-being derive from popular and institutional perceptions that authority is genuine and effective and that it uses morally correct means for reasonable and fair purposes. These qualities are developed, sustained, and enhanced by appropriate behavior over time. The intent would be to generate popular opinion to the effect that life is good or can get better. Implementing this extraordinary set of challenges will not be quick or easy. It will, however, be far less demanding and costly in the political, social, military, and monetary terms than allowing the problems of irresponsible governance and political instability to continue to fester and generate crises that work toward the detriment of all concerned.

What Success and Failure Teach Us about State Failure and the Ultimate Threat to National and International Security

We find that what really perpetrates failure is that the general effort is not well planned, organized, cooperative, coordinated, or conducted over time with cognitive political-psychological skill. As a consequence, (1) strategic ambiguity is introduced; (2) belligerents are given the opportunity to "play at the seams" of the operation and frustrate objectives; (3) allies are allowed to pursue their own particular agendas; (4) political, personal, and monetary costs are increased; and (5) "mission creep" increases the possibilities of mission failure. The political-military lack of real success in Iraq and Afghanistan is a clear reminder that trying to do good things is not as much futile as exceptionally complicated. Success is a product of shrewd planning and implementation, not wishful thinking. Declaring victory and going back home prematurely is a sure formula for failure.[5] The question, then, is "Planning for what?" The answer is straightforward and found in an examination of the contemporary security dilemma.

THE CONTEMPORARY SECURITY DILEMMA

The traditional security dilemma was "What is defense? What is aggression? What is protective action? What is legitimate preventative action?" The answers to these questions have never been completely worked out. In any event, however, there never has been and still is no international entity powerful enough to define and enforce "defense," "aggression," and "protection." It really depends on who, after the fact, writes the history—that is, indeed, a dilemma. The main problem in this context is twofold: (1) the ways and means of achieving or destroying security (i.e., sustainable peace) are unrestricted and, once again, (2) international law is not enforceable.

In the 1990s, however, the secretary general of the United Nations, Boutros Boutros-Ghali introduced two new types of threats, in addition to traditional military offensive and defensive actions, into the global security arena. They are as follows: (1) hegemonic-violent/belligerent nonstate actors (e.g., insurgents, transnational criminal organizations, terrorists, private armies, militias, and gangs) that are taking on roles that were once reserved exclusively for traditional nation-states and (2) indirect and implicit threats to stability and human well-being such as unmet political, economic, and social expectations (e.g., root causes). Accordingly, over a relatively short period of time, the concept of state and personal security became more than simple control of territory and people. Sovereignty would also become the responsibility of the international community to protect and/or prevent peoples from egregious harm. Interestingly and importantly, this broadened concept of security ultimately depends on eradicating the causes as well as the perpetrators of instability.[6]

The new security dilemma, as a result, is more than a question of determining what aggression is and what it is not. To broaden and complicate the issue, the security dilemma now becomes an all-inclusive circular set of questions regarding (1) why, when, and how to intervene to protect people (i.e., personal and collective security); (2) how and when to prevent egregious human suffering; (3) how and when to develop the conditions that lead to political-economic-social development; and (4) how and when to develop responsible state sovereignty and a sustainable peace—and back to simple personal and collective security? These questions, in turn, encompass more than a redefinition of stability/security. Again, this is nothing less than a redefinition of sovereignty. Sovereignty was, in the past, the control of territory and the people in it. Sovereignty has also become the responsibility to prevent illegitimate exploitation of peoples and protect them and their general well-being.[7] This security dilemma is further complicated by the fact that the perpetrators and exploiters of insecurity and instability are not the sum total of the contemporary security dilemma. There are two more really hard problems: (1) dealing with the "root causes" and (2) the problem of having to deal with substantively different types of irregular "perpetrators and exploiters" of "root causes." Any one given type of countereffort does not fit all.

A Cautionary Note

The main element of the U.S. foreign policy, military management, and public diplomacy must sooner or later go beyond the old ad hoc military-centric principle of protection and prevention to the new selective people-centric principle of responsible sovereignty. In this context, sooner or later policy-makers and decision-makers must add another set of questions to the conventional "who, what, why, and so what?" questions. The new set of questions would be, "What might happen *if* the United States should or should not undertake any given type of remedial international action?" Clausewitz argued that this is the first of all strategic questions and the most comprehensive. With that "foreknowledge," the political leader and commander can establish the kind of action on which they are embarking—neither mistaking it for nor trying to turn it into something that it is not.[8] Then, they can ask, "What is the geostrategic end state?" and "*How* can one achieve that most important objective?"

These tasks require that decision makers be very careful and selective in choosing *if* and *how* to become involved in any given conflict situation. The general rule would be that policy makers and decision makers must carefully calculate gains and losses, and when the case warrants, they should intervene earlier rather than later. If done earlier, the initial and intense use of low-cost diplomatic and civilian instruments of statecraft and military support units can be utilized to ensure legitimacy and stability. If done later, the initial and intense use of high-cost military combat units will generally be applied to a losing situation. Ultimately, however, the only test for involvement whatever its form and level is national self-interest. That is the only morality within the anarchy of contemporary world disorder.[9]

TOWARD A PARADIGM FOR CONTEMPORARY SECURITY POLICY

Political and military leaders and opinion makers all over the world have been struggling with these ambiguous political-psychological aspects of conflict since at least the end of the Cold War. Yet, the nature of the contemporary conflict phenomenon is still not well understood. Many influential Western leaders tend to think of the legalistic and military dictums generated from the Treaty of Westphalia and their own relatively limited experience as the only guidelines concerning contemporary conflict that are worth considering. Strategic theory and logic have played little part in the debates and actions that define conflict as a whole. As a consequence, nonstate actor violence and traditional nation-state military response seem to remain the methods of choice in terms of achieving one's geopolitical security ends.

Three Practitioner's Views Regarding the Problem of Contemporary Global Security

In *The Sling and the Stone*, Colonel T. X. Hammes (Ret., U.S. Marine Corps) reminds us that modern asymmetric war involving nonstate actors (i.e., Fourth-Generation Warfare—4GW) is the only kind of war the United States has ever lost. 4GW is an evolved form of insurgency rooted in the fundamental precept that superior political will, when properly employed, can defeat greater military and economic power. It uses all available networks—political, economic, social, informational, and military—to convince enemy decision makers that their strategic goals are either unachievable or too costly to justify the perceived benefits. Using various networks, 4GW directly attacks the minds of enemy decision makers, policy makers, and opinion makers to destroy their political will. Thus, the importance of the media in manipulating public opinion and leadership in changing an opponent's position on a matter of national interest is highly significant.[10]

Additionally, General Rupert Smith (Ret., UK) postulates that contemporary wars are, generally, fought against enemies who are firmly embedded in the population and cannot present a traditional strategic or operational target. No conventional act of force can ever be decisive. Winning a trial of military strength will not deliver the will of the people. Fundamentally, gaining the will of the people is the only effective objective of any use of force in modern war. The reality of contemporary conflict and a new paradigm is that information is the currency on which war is conducted. Thus, both General Smith and Colonel Hammes advocate a transformation in thinking and planning necessary to conduct a successful asymmetrical (i.e., hybrid) war. These empirical observations begin the process of paradigm change. That takes us beyond doing "something" for something's sake. That takes us beyond developing budget, force structure, and equipment packages for a given situation. That also takes us beyond asking: "What are we going to do?" and "Who is going to command and control the effort?" These imperatives take us to well-thought-out, cooperative, collegial, and holistic planning that, in turn, leads to the accomplishment of a twenty-first-century geostrategic end game.[11]

And, in these terms, Ambassador David C. Miller, Jr. recalls, "We worked hard to develop and implement a coherent theory of engagement to contain an expansionist Soviet Union. A great deal of intellectual energy, including national debate and writing, to say nothing of war gaming, went into the question of how and under what circumstances the United States should and could deal with the Soviet Union." Now, Ambassador Miller advocates that the United States must seek to understand new types of enemies and new strategic problems. Moreover, the United States must be able to deal with more than television images and the symptoms of global instability. Lastly, the ambassador advocates that all the actions recommended here must be preceded by clear, holistic, and logical policy direction—and the ends, ways, and means of strategic vision necessary to ensure the achievement of the geostrategic ends established in that policy. The days of delineating a successful strategic end state as a simple exercise in protection of interests or short-term compassion for a humanitarian problem are over. The American public is beginning to expect U.S. efforts, especially if they involve the expenditure of large amounts of tax revenue or the expenditure of even a few American lives, to "make the world a better place."[12]

The main task in the search for security now and for the future, then, is to construct stability and well-being on the same strategic pillars that supported success and effectiveness in the past. The first pillar of success is a conceptual requirement—that is, to develop a realistic game plan, strategic vision, philosophy, or theory of engagement to deal with the contemporary central strategic problem of illegitimate malgovernance around the world today. The second pillar is an organizational requirement to create the planning and management structures to establish as complete a unity of effort as possible to plan and implement that theory of engagement. The third is an organizational and operational requirement. Organizationally, it involves developing and implementing an appropriate combination of political, economic, informational, moral, and coercive instruments of national and international power to pursue the multidimensional requirements of the contemporary global security environment. Operationally, it involves learning to understand friends as well as adversaries and assessing potential adversaries culturally, so as to better influence their thoughts and behaviors. The entire geopolitical effort involves training and educating leaders at all levels to implement a relevant theory of engagement. Addressing anything less than this admittedly massive strategic-level task only addresses symptoms of the problem, not the problem itself.[13]

Ambassador Stephen D. Krasner's Solution to the Problem

Given the long tradition of war between or among nation-states adhering to generally accepted rules and practices initiated with the Peace of Westphalia in 1648, it is hard to equate the multidimensional responsibility to protect (i.e., responsible sovereignty) concept with conventional war, say nothing of understanding how to respond to it. That has been considered too hard, too complex, too ambiguous, and too costly. This broadened definition of the contemporary security problem makes the concept so vague as to render it useless as an analytical tool. The genius of Ambassador Stephen D. Krasner, however, helps clarify the problem.

The theoretical basis for advocating a single orienting principle (i.e., responsible sovereignty) begins with Professor David Easton's now universally accepted and radically innovative definition of politics—that is, "the authoritative allocation of values for a society." In these terms, politics refers to a separable dimension of human activity—that is, legitimate governance. The state and its governance—or lack thereof—becomes the primary (i.e., dependent) variable and defining element in operationalizing the concept of contemporary security. It also makes the concept of legitimate governance intellectually manageable and analytically useful.

Thomas Homer-Dixon, a leading authority in socioenvironmental-political studies, further elaborates the issue. He explains that the role of governance in shaping a society's response to socioeconomic-political-environmental stressors is the critical variable in determining security or insecurity, stability or instability, development or nondevelopment, prosperity or poverty, and back again to peace (i.e., security) or conflict. Without the guarantee of legitimate state-administered control of the national territory and the people in it, every other form of security is likely to remain elusive. Legitimate governance, thus, provides the theoretical foundation for Krasner's orienting principle for foreign policy and power asset management and a "safer and more just world."[14]

Even though Krasner's orienting principle of responsible sovereignty is intellectually manageable and analytically useful, it is not a simple concept. He cautions us that his orienting principle differs from one motivated by a proverbial "wish list" in four ways. First, and most importantly, an orienting principle focuses on specific limited but actionable issue areas. Second, policy based on an orienting principle is distinct from ad hocery—it aspires to something beyond short-term or mid-term material or political interests. Third, the frame offered by the principle of responsibility is that it is a necessary condition for stability, development, prosperity, and a sustainable peace. And, fourth, there may be no specific formula (i.e., model or recipe) that can be applied literally to any given situation. Particular local conditions at any given time will dictate a given action. Thus, the selective use of innovative combinations of soft and hard power over time is an absolute must in contemporary conflict situations.

Ambassador Krasner and others also warn us that intervening powers must also apply the principle of responsible sovereignty with the understanding that they cannot bring about liberal democratic states overnight. Experience reminds us that social engineering projects are best undertaken by the internal actors working on a foundation of moral legitimacy. Moreover, objectives need to be tempered to match both local and international political constraints. Outsiders and domestic leaders must rely on local customs, politics, and practices to establish new institutions that can move over the long term toward international norms of accountable, transparent, legitimate, and democratic governance.

As a consequence, the earliest phases of an intervention must include a transition strategy—not an exit policy. Transition requires clearly delineated political and economic milestones, so that international and local authorities can focus on the challenges of developing the necessary conditions for reconstruction, political reconciliation, socioeconomic development, and the professionalization and modernization of the state bureaucracy and security institutions. Otherwise, declaring victory, going back home, and leaving the country without consistent and vigilant guidance has been known to precipitate corrupt regimes that protect themselves rather than the people of the country. At the same time, the nation's wealth finds its way into the pockets of political or military elite rather than into the socioeconomic development of the country. This takes us back to the threat of state failure and its aftermath. It is a zero-sum game in which nonstate actors and/or corrupt individual actors are the winners—and the rest of the society and the global community are the losers.[15]

The Resultant Peace-Security Paradigm

As noted in Chapter 1, the fulfillment of a holistic, population-centric, legitimate governance and stability-security equation for national and global security consists of three principal elements. They are derived from the independent variables that define security (i.e., S). These three primary elements are first, the coercive capacity to provide a culturally acceptable level of personal and collective stability (i.e., M); second, the ability to generate socioeconomic-political development (i.e., E); and third, the political competence and rectitude to develop a type of governance to which a people can relate and support (i.e., PC). It is heuristically valuable to portray the relationship among these elements in a mathematical formula: $S = (M + E) \times (PC)$.

The strategic-level application of this paradigm would result in a multidimensional, population-centric understanding of the closely interrelated wars within the general war. These wars include the following: (1) a more or less conventional military "war" against a state or nonstate adversary, (2) a "war" to unify a multidimensional effort within the defending or attacking actor's organizational structure that deals with conflict, (3) an "information war" to convince the populace and international public opinion of the moral rectitude of a given campaign, (4) a "war" to isolate an internal or external attacker from his or her internal and external support, (5) an "intelligence war" to locate and neutralize the men and women who plan and execute a given conflict, and (6) a "war" for legitimacy and the moral right of a given attacking or defending regime to exist.

The application of the paradigm at the operational level results in a more precise definition of legitimate governance. The five variables that define and explain the legitimizing and strengthening of a regime are as follows: (1) free, fair, and frequent selection of leadership; (2) the level of participation in or acceptance of the political process; (3) the level of perceived governmental corruption; (4) the level of perceived individual and collective well-being; and (5) the level of regime acceptance by the major social institutions. These key indicators of moral legitimacy are not exhaustive, but they statistically explain a high percentage of the legitimacy phenomenon and provide the basic architecture for the actions necessary to assist governments in their struggle to survive, develop, and prosper. As such, these indictors constitute a strong coherent conceptual framework from which policy, strategy, and operational efforts might flow. The degree to which a political actor effectively manages a balanced mix of these five variables enables stability, development, political competence, security, acceptance, and sustainable peace—or the reverse.[16]

LESSONS: A FINAL CAUTIONARY TALE

Once again, the main task in the effort to develop and implement an adequate contemporary theory of engagement is to begin the long-term geostrategic-level processes of developing the sophisticated expertise, organizational architecture, and civil-military power structure necessary to counter the dual threats of hegemonic or violent nonstate actors and to counter the indirect and implicit threats to national and global security and well-being.

- All these must be accomplished on a basis of moral legitimacy and responsible sovereignty as the orienting principle for foreign policy and power asset management.
- This is where our energies should be directed—not by using superior military power to achieve some limited tactical or operational objective.
- None of these is easy or quickly accomplished but much better than the proven-murderous alternatives.
- All these take us full circle back to the peace and security that stability, development, and political rectitude and competence can create.

The eloquent gloominess of Albert Camus reminds us, however, that "if, finally, the conquerors succeed in molding the world according to their laws, it will not prove [anything] but that this world is hell. . . . But hell can endure for only a limited period, and life will begin again one day. History may perhaps have an end; but our task is not to terminate it but to create it, in the image of what we henceforth know to be true. . . . Is it possible eternally to reject injustice, without ceasing to acclaim the nature of man and the beauty of the world? Our answer is yes. This ethic is the only one that lights the way to a truly realistic revolution. This [legitimate governance] revolution is founded on the common dignity of man . . . and which we must now define in the face of a world that insults it."[17]

VIGNETTE: NONSTATE AND STATE ACTORS AS PROXIES—THE AFGHAN MUJAHIDEEN VERSUS THE 40TH RED ARMY

Nonstate actors are now doing things that only the nation-states have been expected to do in the past—that is, despite the variety of differing methods and motives of nonstate players, many are engaged in one common political act—political war. The intent is to control or radically change a government and to institutionalize the acceptance of one's will. Normally, this act is a direct attack on a governing regime by an insurgent or a revolutionary nonstate actor. An insidious variation on that theme perpetrated over the years by nation-states is indirect interstate war that entails an attack against one state by another through the use of nonstate and/or state proxies. This is a ploy to justify the international legal fiction of "plausible deniability"—that is, denial of the fact that a hegemonic nation-state is using unconventional instruments of statecraft to replace, lessen, or inhibit another regime's capability to control its national territory and/or foreign interests. Consequently, we sketch the Afghan Mujahideen model of proxy war against the Soviet 40th Army, 1979–1989. It is a clear reminder that trying to do plausibly deniable things is not as much futile as exceptionally complicated.

Introduction

Lenin articulated the contemporary political vision within which many nonstate and state actors operate. He taught that anyone wishing to force radical political-economic-social change and compel an opponent to accede to his or her will must organize, equip, train, and employ a body of small political agitator groups. His intent was straightforward. If these unconventional and clandestine instruments of statecraft succeed in helping to tear apart the fabric on which a targeted enemy rests, the instability and violence they create can serve as the "midwife of a new social order."[18] On the other hand, if these indirect and less obvious efforts fail, there is a decisive and direct hard instrument of power, which is the armed forces. Interestingly and importantly, it really does not matter whose armed forces might conduct that liberating mission as long as they are willing and capable of performing the task.[19]

This vision is not the exclusive property of Leninists. Anyone can adapt this concept for his or her own purposes. Thus, in any event and in any phase of a revolutionary process, small and large nonstate political agitator organizations can play substantial roles in helping their political patrons prepare to take control of a targeted opponent. As a consequence, others including Mao, Abimael Guzman, and Osama bin Laden have elaborated and refined Lenin's basic political revolutionary model. Nevertheless, the original tenets remain as useful today as in the past. A state actor's or a hegemonic nonstate actor's use of a nonstate actor surrogate avoids making a direct attack on an opponent and eludes being cited in international legal parlance as an aggressor. At the same time, the targeted enemy is forced to operate in accordance with his or her adversary's political logic, not his or her own. This type of contemporary conflict is playing an increasingly sophisticated role in creating multidimensional indirect threats to security, stability, well-being, and effective national sovereignty all around the world today. Accordingly, the set of lessons that should be learned from the experience in Afghanistan, 1979–1989, begins with an examination of the political-historical context of that case. It also provides a valuable guide to those who would like to better understand and deal with the contemporary art of war and the strategy of the weak versus the strong.

The Political-Historical Context

The Soviet application of Lenin's strategic vision in Afghanistan, 1979–1989, can be seen in the events that led up to the Soviet-Warsaw Pact invasion of Czechoslovakia in October 1968. In October 1967, a group of students from Prague's Technical University organized street demonstrations to protest electricity cuts in their dormitories. Calls then and subsequently for "more light" triggered a broader political notion of more light in the minds of the Czech people that extended well beyond the university and its lighting problems. That notion was given more impetus as a result of the violent suppression of these demonstrations. General public discontent and unrest were obvious, and the government concluded that it had to respond to the calls for "more (political) light." Impasse and indecision finally gave way two months later with the election of a reform candidate as the new secretary of the Central Committee of the Czech Communist Party, Alexander Dubcek. Shortly after his election, Dubcek called for a relaxation of press and media censorship and initiated a purge of "hard-liners" from the party and the army. He also called for an action program for further reforms. Thus, the so-called Prague Spring (with more light) had begun with strong public consent.

Concern on the part of the Soviet Union regarding the reforms was formally expressed as early as March 21, 1968. At a meeting of the Soviet Politburo in Moscow, it was stated that contamination from the Prague Spring was having an antisocial effect on young Ukrainians. Soon thereafter, similar allegations were reported by Polish and East German leaders regarding the youth in their countries. By July 1968, Soviet and other Warsaw Pact leaders had agreed that the Czech reforms were beginning to move out of party control. As a result, a series of repressive, subversive, and coercive counteractions were initiated in quick succession. In the meantime, the Soviet minister of defense was authorized to prepare a contingency plan for military operations in Czechoslovakia. On July 14, Soviet, Polish, East German, Bulgarian, and Hungarian party leaders sent a "fraternal letter" to the Czech Communist Party warning of the risk of counterrevolution, along with a list of measures expected to be taken. Two weeks later, Soviet and Czech leaders met in a face-to-face discussion in which Dubcek tried to convince Leonid Brezhnev that these reforms were not jeopardizing party control. Brezhnev was not convinced.

The Warsaw Pact then announced the forthcoming military exercises to take place near the Czech borders. On August 13, in a telephone conversation with Brezhnev, Dubcek again tried to convince the Soviet leader that the Czech reforms were not a threat to the social-democratic system. Brezhnev remained unconvinced. Five days later, on August 21, 1969, 500,000 Warsaw Pact troops moved unopposed into Czechoslovakia and the country was occupied.[20] Were he still alive, Lenin would remind us that power provides its own legitimacy.

The parallels between the Soviet invasion of Czechoslovakia in 1968 and the invasion of Afghanistan bring us back to the reality of Lenin's revolutionary model. It takes us from the initial use of a more indirect and benign approach to revolutionary change to a direct and decisive approach to radical political change. That gives stronger meaning to the idea of using "all means" to compel an enemy to accept one's will. The Soviets had tried the soft-power approach in Afghanistan for 60 years. Lenin sent a delegation to Kabul to open diplomatic channels in 1919. Later, the Soviets equipped and trained the Afghan Air Force. By 1978, Soviet-trained personnel composed a third of the country's army officers and a majority of professional and technical positions in the government bureaucracy. Moreover, the communists (i.e., the People's Democratic Party of Afghanistan—PDPA) gained control of the government. By the time of the Soviet invasion in December 1979, Soviet military presence had grown from 350 advisers to more than 3,000.

But, back to the party, the PDPA had been deeply divided since its creation in 1965. The controlling extremist hard-liner faction (i.e., the *Khalq*—the people) and the more moderate reformists (i.e., the *Parcham*—the banner) were mortal enemies. At first, the Soviets were enthusiastic regarding the communists taking control of the Afghan government and tried to get the two factions to work together. By March and April 1978, however, the mutual animosity of the *Khalq* and the *Parcham* had begun to create great concern in Moscow. In March 1979, a major uprising took place in the largest city in the west of Afghanistan. Local army forces defected in mass to the *Parcham*. On April 27, 1979, antigovernment forces in the army staged a *coup d'etat* (i.e., also called the April Revolution) that allowed the *Parcham* to take control of about half the country. The Soviets were still urging intraparty unity as late as the middle of October.

In the meantime, the Soviet Ministry of Defense was instructed to develop plans for a military intervention in Afghanistan. In October 1979, the leader of the *Parcham* faction of the PDPA was murdered on the order of the leader of the *Khalqs*. The extremism of the *Khalqs* had become an almost constant problem for those in Moscow who were trying to keep Afghanistan in the Soviet orbit. Things were getting out of control. Over the course of the fall of 1979, the Soviets decided that the leader of the *Khalqs* had to be replaced. Then, in early December 1979, the head of the

KGB (i.e., Committee for State Security) reported to Brezhnev that he believed that the gains of the April Revolution were at risk. Afghanistan was in danger of falling to the West. On December 12, 1979, Brezhnev and senior Politburo members signed a document authorizing military intervention into Afghanistan. On December 24, 1979, the 40th Red Army invaded that country with an expeditionary force of approximately 80,000 men. At the height of its strength, the army numbered about 110,000.[21]

The "Who, Why, What, and How?" Findings

The Soviet invasion of Afghanistan that began in December 1979 was intended to reinstate a puppet regime. That move produced an intransigent opposition of nationalist insurgents and anticommunist religious zealots—the Mujahideen. They did the only thing they could do. They mounted a classic insurgency against the invaders. The Mujahideen were hopelessly divided, however, and remained fragmented for the duration of the conflict. That remained the case even after victory was declared. The Soviet invasion also caused some foreign reactions. The U.S. president Jimmy Carter and his successor, Ronald Reagan, supported and escalated overt and covert assistance to the Mujahideen and other Soviet enemies all around the world. Additional and significant financing, training, and armaments were provided by Pakistan and Saudi Arabia. Other external players included the United Kingdom, China, Egypt, and Iran. That response to the Soviet aggression in Afghanistan came to be seen as a cunningly crafted instrument of U.S. statecraft that bankrupted and ultimately broke the Soviet Union. That may be true, but it was Pakistani general and head of state Muhammad Zia-ul-Haq who put the U.S., Pakistani, and Saudi Arabian coalition together and created the essential unity of effort that enabled the Mujahideen to win the proxy war against Soviet aggression.

To be sure, the United States and other state actors were invaluable partners in the war against the Soviets but they wanted their actions to remain more or less covert—that is, they wanted to be able to claim "plausible deniability" under the long-standing rules of international politics. The Mujahideen and Pakistan would act as U.S. and Arabian proxies in the conflict. Lastly, in all fairness, it should be noted that Brezhnev and the Soviet leadership forgot or ignored the more recent French and American lessons in Vietnam and Algeria. They remembered their decisive success in Czechoslovakia in 1968. As a consequence, and in reality, the Afghan war against the Soviets was not Carter's or Reagan's war, Charlie Wilson's war, or King Saud's war. It was not even the Mujahideen's war, although they did the greater part of the fighting and dying. It became General Zia's war.

Pakistan could and would not claim "plausible denial." Pakistan exposed itself to serious Soviet and Indian reprisals. Taking those risks, Zia insisted that support to the Mujahideen from his nation-state partners came exclusively and clandestinely through Pakistani hands. Pakistan would be the entity that provided the advice, training, equipment, money, safe havens, and advocacy in the international security arena that would ultimately enable the Mujahideen to force the withdrawal of the 40th Red Army and the collapse of the Soviet-backed Afghan regime a few years later.[22]

The Main Enemy and Its Civilian Allies

The direct Soviet intervention in Afghanistan was initially envisioned as a short-term effort to (1) bring stability to a communist-controlled regime that had devolved into a fractious fraternal competition for power, (2) keep Afghanistan in the pro-Soviet power bloc that protected a southern border of the USSR, and (3) retain Afghanistan as a compliant ally within the global competition for ideological acceptance. The primary instrument of statecraft chosen to accomplish those strategic objectives was the Soviet 40th Red Army.

For the Mujahideen, thus, the main enemy was the 40th Red Army. That army represented a foreign and atheistic enemy whose expressed objectives were to change everything that Afghanistan had been for the past several hundred years. As a consequence, the Afghans mounted a classic nationalist and *jihadist* insurgency against the invader. There were only a few set-piece battles. When directly confronted, the Mujahideen simply melted away into the mountains. Territory did not really change hands except for limited periods of time until the Russians moved back to garrison. There was no central command for the Russians to degrade or disintegrate. There were no lower headquarters for the Russians to attack. There were no large units to turn the enormous firepower of the 40th Army against. There were no factories producing arms to bomb. In short, there were no objectives that a highly mechanized and tank-heavy conventional army could successfully target. And, importantly, Russian officers and generals were not prepared to conduct a guerrilla war. They had been trained to fight a conventional war with an emphasis on tank battles against North Atlantic Treaty Organization (NATO) forces in Europe.

Under these circumstances, the Soviets violated elementary principles of humanity. As an example, millions of mines were dropped into Afghanistan or placed by hand. Many were small antipersonnel mines intended to wound or kill civilians and many were disguised as toys in order to tempt children to pick them up. Additionally, when the city of Kandahar rebelled against the Russian occupation in early 1980, they responded by carpet bombing the city. Kandahar was not unique. In sum, the Soviets conducted a military war of terror that did everything possible to alienate the Afghan people and encourage the Mujahideen in the insurgency effort. The Russians would win all the battles and still lose the war. And, the Soviet 40th Army would be completely ineffective in achieving its objectives. Again, the primary geopolitical objective was to restore political power to a loyal communist regime in Kabul.

The enemy lacked proper training and equipment for a guerrilla war. The puppet communist government and the Russian advisers in Kabul were not a lot of help either. Infighting within the PDPA was rampant and sometimes very violent. The results prevented the party from achieving any kind of unity of effort and eroded whatever moral legitimacy they might have had. Those rivalries and the resultant disunity in government were mirrored within the Soviet leadership. Interservice and interagency competition between the military, the Ministry of Foreign Affairs, and the KGB generated struggles for influence and power. The heads of these organizations acted autonomously and dysfunction trickled down to the operational and tactical levels, as the agents and soldiers in the field disagreed over how to conduct a given task. These disagreements allowed the Afghan communists to play various sides against each other and to develop lobbies of their own in Moscow. Clearly, the Soviets and the Afghans were not organized to conduct a counterinsurgency war and to develop and coordinate a strategy to deal with it. Accordingly, the Russians were never able to overcome the Mujahideen. That, as much as anything, contributed to the eventual withdrawal of the 40th Red Army from Afghanistan in 1989 and the demise of the Soviet-backed regime in Kabul a few years later.[23]

The Counterforce: The Mujahideen and Their Pakistani Ally

Riedel, with access to President Carter's diary, asserts that the major objectives of the war early on were to (1) arm and fund the Afghan Mujahideen, (2) use Pakistan as a safe base for the Mujahideen, (3) enlist Saudi help in the war, and (4) turn Afghanistan into a Russian Vietnam. By the end of the Carter presidency, the secret war in Afghanistan was well underway. All the strategic fundamentals were in place. The CIA, ISI (i.e., Pakistan's equivalent to the American CIA), and the GID (i.e., Saudi Arabia's equivalent to the CIA) were actively assisting the Mujahideen in their war against the Soviet 40th Army. Later, President Reagan would escalate the war and make use of Pakistan's general Zia and his country's human and physical resources more fully than President Carter had.

In the meantime, and as indicated earlier, the Mujahideen were badly divided. The Afghan political landscape was wrought with ethnic rivalries, religious tensions, age-old blood feuds, a disjointed tribal system, and strong personal ambitions. All these social divisions overlaid a century-old sociopolitical order based on unwritten social codes and patronage networks. Many of the core tenets of Russian communism were at odds with that Afghan identity. In that context, the atheism that was a part of the communist ideology was highly offensive, and the attack on Islam became an attack on the Afghan identity as well. Thus, the war against the Russian 40th Army became a righteous struggle between good and evil, as well as a nationalistic effort to oust the unwanted foreign occupiers. As a result, the political leaders and their organizations backed by the Soviets were unable to garner sufficient moral legitimacy for their regimes to govern effectively.

Again, as noted earlier, the Mujahideen wanted the Russians out of Afghanistan. Many also wanted to return to a traditional Islamic system of governance. Others advocated other objectives. In the process of trying to accomplish their various sociopolitical ends, the insurgents took heavy casualties and the associated violence produced an unconscionable number of deaths, internally displaced persons, and international refugees. In the general scheme of things, however, the Mujahideen and their specific objectives did not matter much. Without organization and resources, they would be exploited and used as proxies by the three traditional nation-states, each with related but different motives. Again, those states included not only the United States and Pakistan but also Saudi Arabia.

Mujahideen disunity and the legitimacy problem forced General Zia to initiate several activities and political groups intended to generate a minimum level of legitimacy and organize a guerrilla fighting force that could effectively challenge the 40th Red Army. Thus, ISI managed the training of the Mujahideen, selected Soviet targets to attack, and determined which Mujahideen commanders to aid and with how much. The supply line from Pakistan into Afghanistan provided less than 10,000 tons of material a year up to 1983 but, by 1987, the total came up to 65,000 tons a year. Training also began on a small scale. Roughly, 3,000 insurgents went through ISA training camps in the first three years of the war. Then, over the period from 1983 to 1987, some 80,000 "freedom fighters" were trained by ISI instructors. Undeniably, logistic experts, trainers, advisers, and other professionals did not always work in Pakistan. In order to assure that the Mujahideen were capable opponents of the Russian army, small groups of Pakistani officers were sent to Afghanistan out of uniform and with no identifying documentation or material. As the war proceeded, larger groups of ISI-controlled operators would be sent to Mujahideen units. As time went on and as conditions would allow, Pakistani Special Force groups were known to participate with carefully selected Mujahideen units in specific operations. Thus, it was covert and small groups of Pakistani "boots on the ground" that allocated money, equipment, and professional leadership to anti-Soviet and pro-Pakistani insurgents.

The reasoning for this Pakistani effort was fourfold. First, like President Carter, General Zia wanted to turn Afghanistan into a Russian Vietnam. This would preclude the Soviets from organizing any kind of serious threat to Pakistan. Second, and closely related to the first motive, this would preclude the Russians from joining with India in a two-pronged invasion and dismemberment of Pakistan. Third, and again closely related to the first two motives, this would preclude Russia from achieving its age-old objective of securing a warm water port on the Arabian Sea. Lastly, General Zia felt a strong obligation to Islam. The degradation and withdrawal of the 40th Red Army from Afghanistan would also facilitate the conditions for the evolution of Islamic governance in the region.[24]

The Providers of Arms and Money: The United States and Saudi Arabia

President Reagan's second term in office would see a fundamental escalation in the Afghan war against the Soviets. The U.S. objective had been to increase the costs of the Russian occupation, not to end it. After William J. Casey had been appointed to head the CIA, the U.S. objectives and activities began to change. He would begin to advocate the idea that the Pakistani-Saudi-U.S. coalition should push for a small but obvious and definitive victory against the Soviet Union. That victory was defined as pushing the Soviets out of Afghanistan. In the mid-1980s, four developments came together to enable that change. They were as follows: (1) Bipartisan support for the war began to increase in the U.S. Congress, (2) the U.S. budget for the war was increased significantly, (3) the Saudi Arabian government reaffirmed its willingness to match the U.S. increase in funding for the war, and (4) the breakup of the Soviet Union was beginning to unfold.

Reportedly, Saudi Arabia's king Saud could not have been more pleased. The new and enhanced strategy to push the Russians out of Afghanistan would only cost him money. As the world's only absolute monarch sitting on zillions of tons of oil, he did not have to concern himself with anything like public opinion, legislative approval, or money. King Saud was, however, seriously concerned about any possible atheistic communist or reformist challenge to his regime. He was also seriously concerned about the future of Islam in the Middle East. Consequently, the king's strategic objectives went beyond the immediate concerns of the United States and Pakistan. They were to (1) assure the continuation of the Saudi monarchy; (2) assure the defeat of the Soviet army in Afghanistan; (3) assure the continuation of the *jihadi* narrative in the Middle East; (4) enhance Saudi position as the primary defender of Islam everywhere, not just the holy places in Arabia; and (5) covertly advance the notion of Saudi responsibility as the vanguard of the Pan-Islamic effort to restore the Islamic empire of the eighth to the fifteenth centuries.

Importantly, the 1979–1989 Afghan War appears to have marked the beginning of a new era. Atheistic communism and Soviet imperialism created the provocation that led to the idea of a new period of Afghan and Islamic nationalism. That nationalism fed the *jihadi* narrative. That resulted in the "Arab Spring." In turn, some scholars and only a few political leaders argue that the Arab Spring initiated a "long war" to resurrect the glories of the eighth-century Caliphate.[25]

Addressing the "So What?" Question: The Outcome

Beyond the unconscionable number of deaths, casualties, refugees, destruction, instability, and insecurity that war brings on peoples and states, the jihadi narrative takes us to the "long war." The Islamic *jihadists* who dream of a return to the eighth through the fifteenth centuries understand that such a dream cannot be fulfilled overnight. Those dreamers also know that this kind of ultimate political objective and the associated global threat cannot be achieved by "shock-and-awe" tactics that can deliver a final victory in a few weeks. They understand that the geopolitical objective of a new Islamic society and Caliphate will be achieved as a result of a deliberate and lengthy struggle that generates the destabilization and slow destruction of opposing states and societies. This is a conflict with an absolute and unalterable objective in which there is nothing to negotiate or compromise on. To be sure, negotiations and compromises may be used as tactics in a given conflict situation but only as a means for gaining time or another tactical or operational convenience. This unlimited objective requires an unrestricted and long war.[26]

At the strategic level, then, *jihadists* might be expected to mount combinations of various types of wars across the entire spectrum of conflict. They will use diverse battlefields and combinations of methods throughout the global community. They will use inexpensive, obsolete, innovative, and captured equipment, weaponry, and other resources. At the same time, *jihadists* will work toward broader support in the Islamic world and in any non-Islamic community that pledges not to attack Muslims or intervene in their affairs. In short, *jihadists* will do what they can do with what they have to move closer to their long-term geostrategic objectives. The objectives that define the long-term geopolitical end state are to (1) take down all governments that are considered apostate or corrupt, one piece of human or geographical territory at a time; (2) recover all territories that were, any time after 711 AD, Islamic; (3) attain regional and global hegemony; and (4) reestablish the Caliphate.[27]

As a consequence, the long war is a total war in terms of scope, geography, and time. Those who wish to live in interesting time may get their wish. The fainthearted need not apply.

KEY POINTS AND LESSONS

Key Points

- Nonstate actors are now doing things that only nation-states have been doing for years. Limited conventional motives and resources can be dramatically expanded through the use of proxies to attack indirectly the nation-states and/or other nonstate actors. The use of proxies is a ploy to justify the international legal fiction of "plausible deniability" that a hegemonic or rogue political actor is attacking another.

- The Soviet invasion of Afghanistan in December 1979 demonstrated the reality of the use of proxies. That invasion was intended to restore an unpopular deposed communist regime on the southern border of the Soviet Union. The outright Soviet aggression to impose a puppet government produced an intransigent opposition (i.e., the Mujahideen) that did the only thing they could do. The Mujahideen mounted a classic insurgency against the Russian invaders and became Pakistani, Saudi, and U.S. surrogates.

- In the general scheme of things, the Mujahideen not only lacked organization for unity of effort, they had virtually no resources. As a consequence, their objectives did not matter much. They were completely available to be used as proxies by three conventional state actors—each with related but different motives.

- The United States, Saudi Arabia, Pakistan, and a few other countries put together a coalition that provided the covert advice, training, equipment, money, safe havens, and advocacy in the global security arena that would over time enable the Mujahideen to force the withdrawal of the 40th Red Army from Afghanistan.

- Through the mid-1980s, the U.S. objectives and activities in the conflict had been to increase the cost of the Soviet invasion and occupation and create a Russian Vietnam. During President Reagan's second term, the U.S. objectives and activities were directed toward achieving a victory against the Soviet Union. That victory was defined as pushing the Red Army out of Afghanistan.

- Saudi Arabia had much longer range objectives. King Saud was concerned about the atheistic communist challenge to the entire Middle East in general and Islam in particular. As a result, he considered the defeat of the Red Army as only a midterm operational objective. He would direct his strategic-level attention toward supporting a Pan-Islamic effort to restore the glories of the eighth through the fifteenth centuries.

- Pakistan's general Zia was also thinking beyond the immediate situation. He was mostly interested in creating and maintaining the conditions that would preclude any kind of Soviet and/or Indian attempt to degrade or dismember his country. Zia also felt a strong obligation toward Islam.

- The 1979–1986 war in Afghanistan marked the beginning of a new war—that is, a "long war" that would create a new era of global Islamic *jihad*. That war is defined as a total war in terms of scope and geography as well as time.

- The justification for taking proxies seriously as important offensive and defensive instruments of statecraft is straightforward. Sun Tzu taught what General Zia practiced—that is, ". . . a State that has perished cannot be restored, nor can the dead be brought back to life. Therefore, the enlightened ruler is prudent and the good general is respectful of that prudence. Thus, the State is kept secure and the army preserved."[28]

Lessons

As the parties, purposes, and means that pertain to contemporary conflict have changed, so have the so-called battlefields. One of these battlefields is indirect interstate war. That entails aggression by one or more nation-states against another through proxies. The Afghan Mujahideen model for proxy war against the Russian 40th Army provides an excellent example of the depth, breadth, complexity, and effectiveness of this type of modern, indirect, belligerent, politicized state and nonstate activities. Regardless of the analytical separation of the different battlefields, all state and nonstate actors involved are engaged in one common political act—that is, political war. The intent is to compel radical change and to institutionalize the acceptance of one's will. Additional strategic-level analytical commonalities in modern battlefields include the absence of formal declarations or terminations of conflict, the lack of an easily identified human foe to attack and defeat, the lack of specific territory to be attacked or held, the absence of a single credible government or political actor with whom to deal, and the lack of a guarantee that any agreement between or among contending actors will be honored. In this fragmented, complex, and ambiguous political-psychological environment, conflict must be considered and implemented as a whole. Accordingly, in becoming involved in nontraditional and greatly enlarged security arena, one must be organizationally and cognitively prepared to deal with proxies as well as other unconventional players operating across the entire spectrum of conflict.

Once again, the power to deal with all these complexities and ambiguities is not combat firepower or the more benign police power. It is, instead, the multilevel, combined, political, psychological, moral, informational, economic, social, police, and military activity that can be brought to bear holistically on the causes and consequences, as well as the perpetrators, of violence. That kind of response will generate stability, political-economic development, and security. The resultant personal and collective well-being is what leads to durable societal peace and security.

CHAPTER 9

Key Points and Lessons: What High Muckety-Mucks and an Enlightened Electorate Should Know about Conflict and Security in the Contemporary Global Security Arena

This final chapter provides an unconventional glossary of lessons for decision makers, policy makers, implementers, opinion makers, and the enlightened electorate. These lessons can help these individuals to understand the architecture of successful—and unsuccessful—practices in the global security arena. These successes and defeats are empirically proven best or worst practices that lead to strategic victories—or defeats. Hopefully, this information might also lead the United States and the West from an unsuccessful military-law enforcement approach to security to a successful multidimensional peace-security paradigm.

Strong empirical evidence illustrates that the essence of any given contemporary threat situation must be to co-opt, persuade, control, and/or compel an adversary's public opinion and political leadership to accept one's will. That defines war. War leads to insecurity, and vice versa. On the other hand, the key to influencing popular perceptions of security and insecurity is to demonstrate that governmental authority does—or does not—serve public needs and is applied in a culturally acceptable manner. That defines security and insecurity. Security leads to peace, and vice versa. This circular and upward or downward conceptualization of peace and war and security and insecurity provides an explanation of victory and/or defeat. Clearly, interestingly, and importantly, all these apply equally to the "bad guys" as well as the "good guys." Thus, a new spectrum of conflict has emerged. Lessons that should have been learned over the past several years teach us that the winner of any given contemporary conflict is the proverbial last man standing. As a consequence, victory goes to the person who writes the history. Hopefully, he or she is a good person.

In the interviews for the SWORD project, astonishingly, more than 200 respondents explained their success or defeat as a result of luck. The argument was that "luck is an agile spirit that jumps both ways in double quick time. All that matters is that luck should run good on the last throw." As an example, a frequent explanation for the French defeat in Algeria, the British loss of Aden, and the American embarrassment in Vietnam was that they tended to rely on hard military power, sophisticated technology, and luck. Luck simply ran bad on the last throw. This is not a recent issue. In his fourteenth-century discussions on *fortuna* (i.e., luck), Niccolo Machiavelli pointed out that Julius Caesar's successful campaigns in Gaul and elsewhere were not the result of letting *fortuna* go its own unencumbered way. Caesar and his officers worked hard, consistently, and prudently to force luck to jump in Rome's favor at every opportunity. They managed the problem very carefully, deliberately, and with *prudenza* (i.e., prudence). These were the crucial factors at work in Gaul and elsewhere—not luck.

Notes: See Carl von Clausewitz, *On War*, ed. and trans. Michael Howard and Peter Paret (Princeton, NJ: Princeton University Press, 1976, Orig. Pub., 1832), pp. 75–93; Michael Howard, *The Causes of War and Other Essays* (Cambridge, MA: Harvard University Press, 1983), p. 109; John Fishel and Max Manwaring, *Uncomfortable Wars Revisited* (Norman, OK: University of Oklahoma Press, 2006), pp. 57–70; Niccolo Machiavelli, *The Art of War* (New York: Da Capo Press, 1965), pp. 7–8, 84–85, 122–123; and Sun Tzu, *The Art of War*, trans. Samuel B. Griffith (Oxford: Oxford University Press, 1963), pp. 63–64, 77–78.

So, here are a few more "lessons learned" to help *fortuna* jump one's way.

1. SOVEREIGNTY AND SECURITY

As a result of the Treaty of Westphalia in 1648, sovereignty (i.e., control of territory and the people in it) was defined as national security. Nation-state intervention into the domestic or foreign affairs of another nation-state was defined as aggression. Aggression was further defined as "protective" or "preventative." All these were confined to nation-states. Nonstate actors and minor powers were considered nonentities. The primary aggressive or defensive effort was military—perhaps with economic sanctions and/or diplomatic support. The security dilemma was "What is aggression?" "What is defense?" "What is a potential adversary's intention?" "What is protective and what is preventive action?" In the late 1990s, the secretary general of the United Nations identified two new types of threats in addition to traditional protection and/or prevention. They are (1) hegemonic or violent nonstate actors that are taking on roles once reserved exclusively for traditional nation-states, and (2) indirect and implicit threats to stability and human well-being such as unmet political-economic-social expectations (e.g., root causes of instability). Thus, security was redefined as stability. Stability depends on legitimate political-economic-social development and becomes an all-inclusive circular and positive upward process of interdependent relationships among the following: (1) personal and collective well-being of citizens, (2) political-economic-social development, (3) effective and responsible governance, (4) sustainable internal peace, and (5) back to personal and collective security again. The new security dilemma, as a result, is more than determining what is aggression and what it is not. It is a redefinition of sovereignty. Sovereignty is now conditional. It is the responsibility to generate the political competence and moral rectitude that can and will manage, coordinate, and sustain viable national development. That enables the individual and collective well-being that defines stability. That stability is the foundational cornerstone on which security and a sustainable peace is built. Thus, security and stability are often considered to be synonymous. Nevertheless, to be quite correct, stability is the fundamental cornerstone on which security is built—that is, without stability, there can be no security, and vice versa. That is a circular situation in which each part of the equation is dependent on the other. It is no wonder that there is some confusion here.

Notes: See Notes 1, 2, 3, 4, and 11, Chapter 1.

2. THE CIRCULAR NATURE OF THE SECURITY-PEACE PARADIGM

Clearly, the independent variables noted earlier are the pragmatic foundations for national and global well-being. These variables are also the fundamental elements that define the social contract between a people and their government. Leaders who understand this also understand that these closely related variables operate in a circular pattern. Again, that is peace and security, stability and development, responsible governance and effective sovereignty, and back again to peace and security. This pattern seems to take us around and around, again and again. To be more than temporarily effective, however, the circular nature of the peace-security equation requires the development of an upward (positive) spiral. Security also depends on the continuing and expanding development of a country's socioeconomic-political infrastructure. Within this context, a morally honest and competent governing regime can and must generate a continuing and improving upward spiral moving toward a higher and better level of peace and security. Otherwise, with no improvement in personal and collective well-being and relatively no socioeconomic-political development, a situation is created that would be, in fact, a downward and negative movement toward state failure and its aftermath.

Notes: See Notes 1, 2, 3, 4, and 11, Chapter 1.

3. INTERNATIONAL LAW

In the absence of an international "sovereign" to enforce international law and despite the few efforts to provide greater authority to the United Nations to protect populations from abuse and harm, nation-states themselves are supreme. Their only restrictions are the rights and authorities they themselves cede to international organizations such as the United Nations and International Court of Justice. In this context, there are only three rules: (1) traditional international law is not enforceable, (2) only the foolish fight fair, and (3) national self-interest is the only morality within the anarchy of the world order.

Notes: See General Wesley K. Clark (Ret., U.S. Army), *Don't Wait for the Next War* (New York: Public Affairs, 2014), p. xvii; Ambassador George F. Kennan, "Morality and Foreign Policy," *Foreign Affairs*, Winter 1985–1986, pp. 205–218; and Ralph Peters, "Constant Conflict," *Parameters*, Summer 1997, p. 20; Ralph Peters, "The Culture of Future Conflict," *Parameters*, Winter 1995, pp. 18–27.

4. WHAT WAR IS

Just as the world has evolved from an industrial society to an information-based society, so has the warfare. A protagonist does not attempt to win by defeating an enemy's military forces. Contemporary conflict is an evolved form of insurgency rooted in the fundamental precept that superior political will, when properly employed, can defeat greater military and economic power. The protagonist uses all available political, economic, social, informational, and military networks to convince the enemy public and its decision makers that their strategic goals are either unachievable or too costly for the perceived benefits. The better a protagonist is at conducting that persuasive-coercive effort, the more effective that player will be relative to the opposition. Accordingly, the contemporary primary center of gravity changes from a familiar military concept to an ambiguous and uncomfortable political leadership and public opinion paradigm. At the same time, it must be remembered that compulsion of any kind still defines war.

Note: See Colonel T. X. Hammes (Ret., U.S. Marine Corps), *The Sling and the Stone* (Grand Rapids, MI: Zenith Press, 2006), pp. i, 209–210, 246–257.

5. WHAT WAR IS NOT

Conventional wars of attrition no longer exist. Nonetheless, confrontation, conflict, and combat undoubtedly exist all around the world.

Note: General Rupert Smith (Ret., UK), *The Utility of Force: The Art of War in the Modern World* (New York: Alfred A. Knopf, 2007), pp. 3, 415.

6. WAR IS CHANGING

War is no longer limited to using military violence to bring about fundamental and radical political-economic-social change. Rather, a combination of means, including state-supported organizations, such as the Argentine *Piqueteros*, might be used to co-opt, urge, and/or compel the nation-state itself to do an internal adversary's will. The contemporary internal security situation is further characterized by unconventional battlefields that no one from the traditional Westphalian school of conflict would recognize or be comfortable with.

Steven Metz and Raymond Millen have identified four different roles that nonstate actors are playing on the contemporary global stage. The first is potentially very dangerous—that is, a nonstate actor acting as a traditional hegemonic nation-state aggressor. The problem for the hegemonic state or nonstate protagonist is that the targeted adversary is likely to be supported by superior conventional forces and cannot be successfully attacked in any kind of conventional kinetic manner. The hegemonic nonstate actor must find a viable indirect substitute for conventional war. Al-Qaeda/Islamic state operations in the Middle East are only one example of what Qiao Liang and Wang Xiangsui call "unrestricted war."

The second type of war is closely related to conventional war. Proxy war or surrogate war is, in fact, indirect state versus state conflict. Nation-states use proxies to do indirectly what might be very risky to do directly under accepted international norms and law. For example, the "Green Men" operating in Ukraine qualify as surrogates for their Russian sponsor. This is another form of unrestricted war.

A third type of violent nonstate activity is insurgency war. That appears to be less a product of radical ideological notions than the problems of malgovernance. Thus, this type of war encompasses direct and indirect actions intended to achieve radical political-economic-social reform. The "wars for national liberation" in Algeria and Vietnam are good examples of insurgency war. This, too, is considered to be an unrestricted war.

The fourth type of violent nonstate conflict comes in very different forms and more than the usual complexity. For lack of a better label, Metz and Millen call this violent and politicized nonstate phenomenon irregular war. Irregular war involves direct and indirect actions against other nonstate actors and, possibly, international players performing mandated tasks based on Chapters 6 and 7 of the UN Charter. Examples of international players dealing with nonstate actors under the UN Charter would include direct UN action against the M23 militias in the Democratic Republic of the Congo and action against gangs in Haiti. Once again, restrictions apply only to the "good guys" and are aptly labeled as unrestricted war.

Notes: Seven Metz and Raymond Millen, *Future War/Future Battlespace: The Strategic Role of American Landpower* (Carlisle Barracks, PA: Strategic Studies Institute, 2000), p. 47; and Qiao Liang and Wang Xiangsui, *Unrestricted Warfare* (Beijing, China: PLA Arts and Literature Publishing House, 1999), title page.

7. WAR IS AMBIGUOUS

The traditional distinctions between crime, terrorism, subversion, and insurgency are blurred. Popular militia, mercenary, gang activity, and warfare are also blurred. Underlying these ambiguities is the fact that most of these activities tend to be the intrastate affairs that international law and convention are only beginning to address. In these conflicts, there is normally no formal declaration or termination of conflict, no easily identifiable enemy military formations to attack and destroy, and no specific territory to take and hold. At the same time, there is no singly credible government or political actor with which to deal or to hold responsible. There are no legal niceties such as mutually recognized borders and Geneva Convention guidance to help control a given situation, no guarantee that any agreement between contending parties will be honored, and no commonly accepted rules of engagement (i.e., ROE) to guide the leadership of any state or nonstate actor.

Additionally, there is no territory that cannot be bypassed or used, no national boundaries or laws that cannot be ignored or used, no method or means that cannot be disregarded or used, and no battlefield (i.e., dimension of conflict) that cannot be ignored or used in some combination. This is why Qiao and Wang call contemporary conflict "unrestricted warfare."

Note: Qiao and Wang, *Unrestricted Warfare*, 1999.

8. EXAMPLES OF AMBIGUOUS (I.E., HYBRID) CONFLICT— COMBINATIONS

Military, political, economic, informational, cultural, and technological (in addition to land, sea, air, space, electronic, biological, and international alliances) dimensions of conflict are all individual battlefields in their own right. For example, economic warfare may be subdivided into trade war, financial war, and sanctions war. At the same time, each dimension or its subparts can be combined with as many others as a protagonist's cognitive abilities, organizations, and resources can deal with. That combining of dimensions provides considerably greater strength (i.e., power) than one or two operating by themselves. This concept can and must be applied in terms of an adversary's political-psychological-military deterrent capabilities. The interaction among the multiple dimensions of conflict gives new and greater meaning to the idea of a state or nonstate action using all available instruments of national and international power to pursue its objectives.

A few examples of military, transmilitary, and nonmilitary warfare would include the following:

- Guerrilla war/drug war/media war
- Conventional military war/network war/financial war
- Biological war/cyber war/terrorist war
- Trade war/information war/intelligence war
- Diplomatic war/ideological war/conventional military war

The notion of combinations within the context of Qaio and Wang's *Unrestricted Warfare* or the work of any other contemporary conflict theorist cannot be considered too ambiguous, too complex, too hard to deal with, or immoral. All of that may be true but to admit that and doing nothing would invite and admit defeat. In turn, such a negative response would likely submit one's posterity to unconscionable consequences. Qaio and Wang would remind us that "a kinder more-gentle war in which brutality and bloodshed may be reduced is still war. It may alter the process of war, but there is no way to change the essence of war, which is one of compulsion, and therefore it cannot alter its cruel outcome either."

Note: Qiao and Wang, *Unrestricted Warfare*, 1999, p. 25.

9. UNRESTRICTED WAR IS TOTAL WAR

Current and future asymmetric conflicts can be total on at least three levels—scope, social geography, and time. In terms of scope and social geography, conflict can now involve entire populations, their neighbors, and friends. Time is also a very comprehensive instrument of power and statecraft. The contemporary "long war" includes no place for compromise or other options short of the ultimate geopolitical objective. Those who want to change history, avenge grievances, find security in new political structures, and/or protect or reestablish old ways are not easily discouraged. They are not looking for anything tangible. They seek the realization of a dream. Negotiations cannot be considered a viable means to end a conflict. Rather, negotiations are tactical and operational-level means for gaining time. Vladimir Ilyich Lenin was straightforward: "Concessions are a new kind of war—outside traditional rules, limitations, and conventional methods." All this is a zero-sum game in which there is only one winner. Again, that is the last man standing. It is, therefore, total.

Note: V. I. Lenin, "Capitalist Discords and Concessions Policy," in Robert C. Tucker, ed., *The Lenin Anthology* (New York: W.W. Norton, 1975), pp. 628–634.

10. WHO AND/OR WHAT IS THE ENEMY?

Experience gained from hundreds of small, uncomfortable asymmetric wars that have taken place over the past half century teaches us that war has indeed changed and is extremely ambiguous. At base, the enemy has now become the political actor who plans and implements the multi-dimensional kinds of indirect and direct, nonmilitary and military, and nonlethal and lethal internal and external activities that threaten a given society's general well-being and exploit the root causes of internal instability.

Accordingly, as noted earlier, in the 1990s, the secretary general of the United Nations introduced two new types of threats—in addition to traditional military-defensive aggression—into the global security arena. They are as follows: (1) hegemonic/violent/belligerent nonstate actors (e.g., insurgents, transnational criminal organizations, terrorists, private armies, militias, and gangs) that are taking on roles that were once reserved exclusively for traditional nation-states, and (2) indirect and implicit threats to stability and human well-being such as unmet political, economic, and social expectations. Accordingly, over a relatively short period of time, the concept of state and personal security became more than simple control of territory and people. Sovereignty (i.e., security) would also become the responsibility of the international community to protect and/or prevent peoples from egregious harm. Importantly, this broadened concept of security ultimately depends on eradicating the causes as well as the perpetrators of instability.

Notes: See Note 1, aforementioned. Also see Boutros Boutros-Ghali, *An Agenda for Peace* (New York: United Nations, 1992); and Boutros Boutros-

Ghali, "Global Leadership after the Cold War," *Foreign Affairs*, March/April 1996, pp. 86–98.

11. WHAT IS THE ENEMY'S PURPOSE/MOTIVE/OBJECTIVES?

One can no longer realistically expect to destroy or capture an enemy's military formations. Enemies now conceal themselves among the population in small groups and maintain no fixed addresses. The nontraditional contemporary goal of becoming involved in a conflict is to establish conditions for achieving strategic geopolitical-psychological objectives. Nontraditional enemies now seek to establish conditions that drain and exhaust their stronger opponents. In striving to establish these destabilizing operational-level conditions, opponents' tactical-level objectives center on attaining the widest freedom of movement and action to operate with impunity and maximize the possibilities for achieving their operational and strategic objectives. Operational-level objectives, then, would include the achievement of short-term and midterm policy goals and establishing acceptance, credibility, and de facto legitimacy within the local, national, and international communities. The geostrategic political motive, whether political, commercial, or ideological, would be to impose one's will on one's adversary. Revolutionary theorist Abraham Guillen warns us that this is a struggle without clemency that exacts the highest political tension.

Note: Abraham Guillen, *Philosophy of the Urban Guerrilla: The Revolutionary Writings of Abraham Guillen*, ed. and trans. Donald C. Hodges (New York: William Morrow, 1973), pp. 278–279.

12. WHAT INTERESTS OR SECURITY/SOVEREIGNTY ISSUES DOES THIS THREATEN?

The objectives noted earlier represent a quintuple threat to the authority, legitimacy, and stability of the targeted governments. Generally, these threats include the following: (1) undermining the ability of a government to perform its legitimizing functions; (2) significantly changing a government's foreign, defense, and other policies; (3) isolating religious or racial communities from the rest of a host nation's society and beginning to replace traditional state authority with alternative (e.g., criminal or religious) governance; (4) transforming socially isolated human terrain into "virtual states" within the host state, without a centralized bureaucracy and with no official easily identified military forces; and (5) conducting low-cost actions calculated to maximize damage, minimize response, and display carefully staged media events that lead to the erosion of the legitimacy and stability of a targeted state's political-economic-social system. The intent is to move the state into the state failure process and exploit the situation for one's own purposes.

The state failure, thus, is not the ultimate threat. Boutros Boutros-Ghali would remind us that the ultimate threat is the coerced transition of extant values of a given society to the values of an unwelcome antagonist. Albert Camus reminds us that Adolph Hitler's attempt to change the international system began as a gang (i.e., the Brownshirts) effort in Munich, Germany. Over a short 12-year period, 1933–1945, Hitler imposed the ethics of a criminal gang on an entire civilization. The resultant World War II was an unconscionable humanitarian disaster that was the sum and substance of the aftermath of contemporary conflict and state failure.

Notes: See Note 4, aforementioned. Also see Albert Camus, *The Rebel* (New York: Vintage Books, 1956), p. 179.

13. IN THIS CONTEXT, IF THE UTILITY OF FORCE IS LIMITED, WHAT IS POWER?

Again, power is no longer simply combat firepower directed at an enemy soldier or industrial complex. Power is multilevel and multidimensional—a combined political, psychological, moral, informational, economic, social military, police, and civil bureaucratic activity that can be brought to bear appropriately against the causes as well as the perpetrators of violence. As an example, it must be remembered that the infamous Berlin Wall was breached with the powerful Deutsche Mark—not aircraft, artillery, armor, or infantry.

This kind of result may be achieved by individuals familiar with Sun Tzu's "indirect approach"—that is, Professor Joseph S. Nye's "smart power." That includes an understanding of diverse cultures, an appreciation of the power of dreams, and mental flexibility that goes well beyond traditional forms. The principal tools in this situation include the following: (1) intelligence operations, (2) public diplomacy at home and abroad, (3) "weaponized" information and propaganda operations, (4) cultural manipulation measures to influence and/or control public opinion and decision-making leadership, and (5) foreign alliances and partnerships. As a consequence, Qaio and Wang stress that warfare is no longer an exclusive "imperial garden" where professional soldiers alone can mingle. Nonprofessional warriors (e.g., hackers, media experts, software engineers, accountants, financiers, biologists, and all kinds of hegemonic nonstate organizations) are posing a greater threat to personal and collective security and stability all around the world today.

Notes: Qiao and Wang, *Unrestricted Warfare*, 1999, pp. 74–75, 117; and Joseph S. Nye, Jr., "Restoring American Leadership through Smart

Power," *Global Strategic Assessment* (Washington, DC: National Defense University, Institute for National Strategic Studies, 2005), pp. 747–476.

14. WHAT IS VICTORY? WHAT IS DEFEAT?

Victory is the sustainable peace generated by the stability, national political-economic-social development, and the morally honest political competence that creates responsible governance and security. It is fairly easy to conceptualize but extremely difficult to operationalize. That takes time, effort, organization, and money. Defeat is easy to operationalize. All that one has to do to operationalize that concept is nothing. Unless thinking and actions are reoriented to deal with that fact, the problems of global security and stability will resolve themselves—there would not be any.

Notes: John T. Fishel and Max G. Manwaring, *Uncomfortable Wars Revisited* (Norman, OK: University of Oklahoma Press, 2006), p. 75; and Jorge Verstrynge Rosas, *La guerra periferica* (Madrid: El Viejo Topo, 2005), pp. 68–87.

15. SUMMARY AND IMPLICATIONS

The concept of contemporary conflict can be summarized by taking a page from a Harry Potter adventure. It can be called Wizard's Chess. It is instructive and sobering.

In that game, protagonists move pieces silently, and subtly, all over the game board. Under the player's studied direction, each piece represents a different type of direct and indirect power and might simultaneously conduct its lethal and non-lethal attacks from differing directions. Each piece shows no mercy against its foe and is prepared to sacrifice itself in order to allow another piece the opportunity to destroy or control an opponent—or to checkmate the King. Over the long-term, however, the game is not a test of expertise in creating instability, conducting violence or achieving some sort of moral satisfaction. Ultimately, it is an exercise in survival. A player's failure in Wizard's Chess is death, and is not an option.

Note: The idea of Wizard's Chess is taken from J. K. Rowling, *Harry Potter and the Sorcerer's Stone* (New York: Arthur A. Levine, 1997), pp. 282–284.

16. A CAUTIONARY NOTE

Sun Tzu prophetically warns us that "war is of vital importance to the State; the province of life or death; the road to survival or ruin. It is mandatory that it be thoroughly studied."

Note: Sun Tzu, *The Art of War*, 1971, p. 63.

Afterword

by Alan D. Manwaring

My invitation to write this afterword stems from an exchange between me and my then three-and-a-half-year-old son, Will, while I made some concluding remarks at my father's Lifetime Achievement Award Luncheon at the Center for a Secure Free Society (SFS Foundation) Western Hemisphere Security Forum in November 2017. Joseph Humire in his introductory remarks at the Lifetime Achievement Award Luncheon (you can go online and see the entire forum) provides some context that may explain why the son of the author is penning the afterword of what may be his final book after a long career of public service in the national security arena and a long list of significant publications, stretching back to 1988 (although, at the age of 86, my father may surprise us—I certainly hope so), but I think it is altogether fitting that I expand to provide even more context.

The father-son relationship I have had with my dad—and continue to have—is quite unique I think, and when asked how this unique relationship started, I think I can identify a dinner held after a book signing event for his book titled *Managing Contemporary Conflict: Pillars of Success* published in 1996. This was at the end of the day when my father and his associates had hosted a small conference intent on discussing many of the issues related to the book followed later by a book signing event that evening at the DACOR House in Washington, DC. At the informal dinner at the end of the day, attended by Ambassador Edwin Corr, Ambassador

David Passage, my father and mother, and me, the conversation began to focus on how the important ideas developed and addressed by my father and his associates needed to get to a broader group of policy makers. I had spent the past several years working on the Hill for a member of Congress and then organizing a Women's Economic Summit as a partnership between the White House and the Kellogg School of Management at Northwestern University, where the premise was to bring together people from the business, academic, and public policy communities to accomplish a designed end. Based on my previous experience, my father asked me to organize a conference related to the publication of his Managing Contemporary Conflict book series. Thus, I became a member of a group of security experts working on national and international security issues.

At some point after listening to my father and his associates talk about how important getting these ideas out to the broader world was, I remarked, "You just had 40 of your closest friends at this conference this afternoon and various others join you at the later book signing—which was wonderful—but if you want to really get your message out to a group of policy makers outside your circle you need to expand your circle and include legislators, business leaders, and academics outside your current world."

Ambassador Corr, the de facto leader of the group, whom I often refer to as "Dad's associates," responded to my remark by saying, "OK, Alan, then when you are done with the project you are currently working on you can take those same principles of bringing together people from the business, academic, and public policy communities and apply them to your father's work." Thus began what has *in essence* become a lifetime mission to take my father's work—concepts and paradigms I have a strong belief in the value thereof—and work to expand their influence in the practical world. *In essence,* taking *a challenge* to work to bring together people from the business, academic, and public policy communities to further the desired end of expanding the practical application of what has become known *at least in part* (and very reluctantly by my father, I might add) as the Manwaring Paradigm.

Fast-forward from that dinner to the event referenced in November 2017 where the SFS Foundation hosted their inaugural Western Hemisphere Security Conference with a theme of preparing future thought leaders in the area of nation security strategy to meet the challenges of "contemporary conflict" so to speak. At that inaugural conference, the SFS Foundation presented my father with a lifetime achievement award and perhaps even more significant than the lifetime achievement award they inaugurated a tradition of recognizing an outstanding individual in national security policy public service with an award named in honor of my father—the Manwaring Award (*the first recipient that year at the inaugural forum was Congresswoman Ileana Ros-Lehtinen—a very distinguished member of the House Foreign Affairs Committee*). At the luncheon where they presented my father with his lifetime achievement award, they asked that I wrap up the luncheon with some very brief comments.

I had three things in mind I wanted to convey in those brief remarks at the conclusion of the luncheon that day. The first was to relate the story of when at the conclusion of an event I accompanied my father to (and over the past twenty-plus years I have accompanied him to *many* events) he was asked by an Army Major or Lt. Colonel the question: what is the most important thing for us to remember (or to know) as we prepare for the next generation of what we are going to be doing? And he immediately responded with "learn history, learn history, learn history." The second was to explain that while growing up in such a unique environment and then becoming something of a cohort in crime with my father and his colleagues my friends would often ask me what my father does and I would simply tell them that from what I can tell *he simply tells people common sense* —which is that if you want to understand how to deal with asymmetric warfare, then you simply need to understand (and deal with) the root causes—and for some reason the world makes a big deal out of that. And the third was to say thank you to so many of those who had been so instrumental, supportive, and helpful in bringing him (us) to the place where he found himself receiving a lifetime achievement award and having an ongoing award for distinguished public service in national security policy named in his honor.

Those were the three ideas I wanted to make sure I conveyed in my brief remarks to close the luncheon, but they apparently paled in comparison to the message that was conveyed when I had an exchange with my three-and-a-half-year-old son, Will, while he accompanied me on the stage for my remarks. While I was attempting to convey my three ideas with Will in my arms he became as uninterested as any three-and-a-half-year-old would at a luncheon focused on national security strategy and kept asking me what more I needed to tell "them." Finally, after several interruptions, I said to Will, "I have to tell them one last thing" to which he responded, "What do you need to tell them?" I looked at Will and said, "I've got to tell them that the most important thing for your generation is to understand—to deal with what they've got to deal with—the root causes of what's going on in the world which are economic and social issues—you've got to understand the root causes of what causes all the problems and if they can understand that then your generation will be in good shape."

For the rest of the afternoon I was told over and over that "Will stole the show" and that his question to me, "What do you need to tell them," and my response directly to him captured the essence of what the forum was intended to be all about.

So, if the question from Will and the direct response to Will are *to be relevant*—for the form where that exchange "stole the show" itself *to be relevant,* for the entire body of work my father has dedicated his life to *to be relevant,* the question then becomes: what is to be done? How can we truly continue in a work that will make the world a safer place for my son Will?

In part the answer surely comes from the announced purpose of the SFS Forum—to continue to prepare the next generation of strategic thinkers. This will only be done by continuing the work of *the challenge* of Ambassador Corr from the dinner in 1996—to expand the practical application of the ideas found in this book and often referred to as the Manwaring Paradigm.

This is the challenge I have taken on for a long time and I remain committed to. And while I can remain committed to the challenge—this is a challenge that will only be accomplished if those who collectively brought us along the path that led to the events of November 2017 at the SFS Western Hemisphere Security Forum continue to be committed to the effort *well after the last publication of my father's work.*

And there have been so many people and institutions that have not just been instrumental *but essential* in bringing us along this path. A path that has admittedly had some bumps and bruises along the way.

The first people that were instrumental in this process were instrumental from before the informal challenge from Ambassador Corr and my father came in 1996. Congresswoman Marjorie Margolies provided me a "Hill experience" quite unique that included insight into understanding the importance of bringing together the business, academic, and public policy communities to achieve anything of significance—it was that guiding principle learned while working with her that guided me in my initial approach to "the challenge." Marjorie's insight coupled with the experience I was having at the Fels Institute of Government at the University of Pennsylvania (where I was then a graduate student) provided the perfect "practicum" education in the importance and significance of reaching out and *genuinely* including all the stakeholders in any endeavor whether it was in business or public policy. John Mulhern and Howard Cohen were two key professors at the Fels Institute who had the insight to not just allow me *but encourage me* to continue in the program at Fels while working with Marjorie in Washington, DC, and then with other projects that applied the idea of bringing together the business, academic, and public policy communities to accomplish a desired end. Besides the encouragement to engage in applying the concepts being taught, the Fels Institute of Government provided significant resources including office space and the such to facilitate some of the initial projects that started me down this *still informal* path.

After the challenge was informally issued by Ambassador Corr, among the first to answer the challenge were the people at Creative Associates International, namely, Charito Kruvant and Steve Horblitt, who hosted and underwrote our first small gathering where we attempted to bring the business, academic, and public policy communities together to talk about the importance of furthering my father and his associate's work—a gathering appropriately titled the *Conference in Search of a National Security Strategy*.

There were then so many other key individuals and institutions that were essential in our continued *informal* path. Key among them were the people at the North South Center at the University of Miami, namely, Ambassador Ambler Moss and Robin Rosenberg; the Center of Hemispheric Policy at the University of Miami, namely, Susan Kaufman Purcell and Susan Davis; the Center for Latin American Issues at the George Washington University School of Business, namely, Jim Ferrer and Ray Marin; the Universidad de Los Andes in Bogota, Colombia, namely, Ambassador Fernando Cepeda and Angela Maria Londono de la Cuesta; the Universidad Francisco Marroquin in Guatemala, namely, Santiago Fernandez Ordonez; and the Universidad Catolica de Chile in Santiago de Chile, namely, General Juan Emilio Cheyre.

The group I often refer to as my father's associates include many. In addition, there are others I would consider *my associates* that have been picked up along the way. Key among them *from my interaction* (my father would certainly include a wider group) include Ambassador Corr (who without doubt has always been the de facto leader of the group); Ambassador David Passage; Norman Bailey; Maria Velez de Berliner; Douglas Farah; Roger Pardo-Maurer; Steve Johnson; Michelle Loosli; Craig Deare; General Julio Hang, Director of the Institute of International Security and External Relations for CARI in Buenos Aries, Argentina; Jay Cope at the Center for Hemispheric Defense Studies at the National Defense University; and Douglas Lovelace, Director of Strategic Studies Institute at the U.S. Army War College.

In addition, there have been several key people who were *for lack of a better term* remnants of my friends from both my undergraduate and graduate educations who have always been encouraging and supportive throughout this informal process and very instrumental in the latest educational program presented by our informal group at the University of Utah; they include Mark Crocket, a JD from Stanford University, and Henry Wurts, a PhD in Risk Management from the Wharton School at the University of Pennsylvania—two of the most brilliant people I have ever known in a world where I have been surrounded by brilliant people. In 2016, at the University of Utah, Taylor Randall, Dean of the Eccles School of Business, along with Jason Perry, Director of the Hinckley Institute of Politics, and Courtney McBeth, also then with the Hinckley Institute, facilitated a conference focused on addressing the importance of combining the various stakeholder communities in working toward a more sound national security strategy.

And *special thanks* must be reserved for Alex Chafuen, President of the Atlas Foundation and Chairman of the Center for a Secure Free Society; Joseph Humire, Executive Director of the SFS Foundation, along with some of the senior fellows and other associates at the SFS Foundation: Fernando Menendez, Jeffery D. Gordon, Jon Perdue, Mark Walker, and Ambassador Curt Winsor; Brian Fonseca, Director of the Jack D. Gordon Institute of Public Policy at Florida International University; Travis Seegmiller, a Partner (Ret.) at Patton Boggs, LLC and currently a professor of Business Law at Dixie State University; our "international partners" Julio Cirino in Argentina and John Griffith and Arturo Contreras in Chile; and most recently Mara Batlin and Nancy Truitt who have been particularly encouraging in working to find a path to continue what they consider the important work of my father.

The list could go on, and in my normal absentminded way, I am sure I have left out someone of major significance who contributed greatly to continuing our informal effort along the path for the past twenty-plus years—but I think the point of including a list of those (as incomplete as it most surely is) who have been so essential in furthering the work and concepts laid out in this book is to address the very real issue that this effort *over the past many years* resulting from the challenge offered in 1996 and encompassed in what is being taught under the banner in some camps as the Manwaring Paradigm has been a *collective* effort—*and most importantly* that for the Manwaring Paradigm or the same concepts stressing the importance of identifying and then addressing the root causes of our security challenges throughout the world *by any other name* to truly be the guidepost in preparing the next generation of strategic thinkers in the area of national security strategy, it *must* continue to be a *collective effort* moving forward from *all* those who had part in bringing us this far in the still *very* unaccomplished mission of working toward the institutional development of an effective national security strategy.

It is now the challenge of this new generation of thinkers—embodied in many of the names listed earlier and led now primarily through the efforts of Humire, Menendez, Gordon, Perdue, Walker, and Fonseca—to work toward enabling us to develop a better national security strategy as a public policy community in a way that *genuinely* includes all stakeholders. That is not an easy task, and as the tasks of my father's generation were and still are multigenerational, so this task is as well.

As what I consider to be at least a part of the responsibility of writing the afterword for what I believe will be my father's last *complete book* publication (although I look forward to him surprising us all), I offer two suggestions on how this new generation of thought leaders must proceed. First, they must focus on continuing and expanding the educational efforts begun by the SFS Foundation in expanding that circle of those trained in the ideas encompassed in what they refer to as the Manwaring

Paradigm—the paradigm requiring that the variable of identifying and addressing root causes in any equation designed to solve security problems facing our country *must* be included to achieve a successful outcome. The second, and equally as important in order to achieve *institutional* impact, will be to work toward the development of a new National Security Strategy Act by Congress that incorporates two major components: first, that of requiring *additional and measurable* cooperation regarding specifically defined strategy between interdepartmental efforts in the federal government—primarily between state, defense, and intelligence; and second, that of requiring that the White House, in issuing its annual National Security Strategy, be required to include defined *ends, ways, and means* of accomplishment.

Neither of these two *suggestions* on how this new generation of thought leaders must proceed to incorporate the ideas outlined in this book and encompassed in my father's lifework (and notably the lifework of many others) will be accomplished overnight. These are challenges that will take a generation, and this new generation of thought leaders cannot accomplish this challenge without the continued efforts of many of those institutions and individuals listed earlier.

But here is the thing—this new generation of thought leaders is well on its way in its efforts to move the security policy community toward institutional development of better security strategy, so that hopefully my now five-year-old son Will's generation will *be in good shape*—able to provide expanded economic and social opportunity to a growing world population yearning to live in a more secure and free society.

It is simply all common sense.

So let's get on with it.

Notes

PROLOGUE

1. Sun Tzu, *The Art of War* (Oxford: Oxford University Press, 1971), pp. 77–78, 144–145.
2. Carl von Clausewitz, *On War* (Princeton, NJ: Princeton University Press, 1976), pp. 72–93, 596.
3. Joseph S. Nye, Jr., "Restoring American Leadership through Smart Power," *Global Strategic Assessment* (Washington, DC: National Defense University, Institute for National Strategic Studies, 2005), pp. 474–476.

CHAPTER 1

1. As an example of the literature see Amos A. Jordan, William J. Taylor, Jr., and Michael J. Mazarr, *American National Security*, 5th ed. (Baltimore, MD: Johns Hopkins University Press, 1999), pp. 3–46; Sam C. Sarkesian, *U.S. National Security* (Boulder, CO: Lynne Rienner Publishers, 1989), pp. 7–8; Lars Schoulz, *National Security* (Princeton, NJ: Princeton University Press, 1987), pp. 24–25, 143–330; Seyom Brown, *New Forces, Old Forces, and the Future of World Politics* (New York: Harper Collins, 1995); and Mohammed Ayoob, "Defining Security: A Subaltern Realist Perspective," in Keith Krause and Michael C. Williams, eds., *Critical Security Studies* (Minneapolis, MN: University of Minnesota Press, 1997), pp. 121–146.
2. Max G. Manwaring, *Ambassador Stephen Krasner's Orienting Principle for Foreign Policy (and Military Management)—Responsible Sovereignty* (Carlisle Barracks, PA: Strategic Studies Institute, 2012), pp. 1–44.

3. Boutros Boutros-Ghali, *An Agenda for Peace* (New York: United Nations, 1992); and Boutros Boutros-Ghali, "Global Leadership after the Cold War," *Foreign Affairs*, March/April 1996, pp. 86–98.

4. Ibid. Also see www.unglobalcompact.org; *Millennium Report: Responsibility to Protect* (New York: International Commission on Intervention and State Sovereignty, August 2001); and http://www.oas.org/en/sms/docs/declaration%20security%20americas%20rev%201%20-%2028%20oct%202003%20ce00339.pdf. Also see Francis M. Deng, et al., *Sovereignty as Responsibility* (Washington, DC: The Bookings Institution, 1996), p. 33; Lee Feinstein and Ann-Marie Slaughter, "A Duty to Prevent," *Foreign Affairs* (Council on Foreign Relations, January/February 2004), pp. 136–150; and Amitai Etzioni, "Responsibility as Sovereignty," *Orbis*, Winter 2006, pp. 1–15.

5. Ibid. Also see Carl von Clausewitz, *On War*, ed. and trans. by Michael Howard and Peter Paret (Princeton, NJ: Princeton University Press, 1976; Orig. Pub. 1832), pp. 80–81, 89, 596.

6. Qiao Liang and Wang Xiangsui, *Unrestricted Warfare* (Beijing: PLA Literature and Arts Publishing House, 1999), pp. 77–78, 109, 144–145; and George F. Kennan, "Morality and Foreign Policy," *Foreign Affairs*, Winter 1985–1986, pp. 205–218.

7. General Rupert Smith (Ret., UK), *The Utility of Force: The Art of War in the Modern World* (New York: Alfred A. Knopf, 2007), pp. 3, 145.

8. Qiao and Wang, *Unrestricted Warfare*, 1999.

9. Krasner, "An Orienting Principle for Foreign Policy," 2010.

10. David Easton, *The Political System: An Inquiry into the State of Political Science* (Chicago, IL: University of Chicago Press, 1971, 1981), pp. 99, 128–129.

11. Krasner, "An Orienting Principle for Foreign Policy," 2010. Also see Amitai Etzioni, "Changing the Rules," *Foreign Affairs*, November/December 2011, p. 173; and Joseph S. Nye, Jr., "Restoring American Leadership through Smart Power," *Global Strategic Assessment* (Washington, DC: National Defense University Institute for National Strategic Studies, 2009), pp. 474–476.

12. Max G. Manwaring and John T. Fishel, "Insurgency and Counter-Insurgency: Toward a New Analytical Model," *Small Wars and Insurgencies*, Winter 1992, pp. 272–310. This research is based on more than 300 interviews conducted by Colonel Alfred W. Baker and Dr. Max G. Manwaring. The individuals interviewed were civilian and military experts with direct experience in 69 post–World War II intranational conflicts. The effort was originally mandated by the vice chief of staff of the U.S. Army, General Maxwell Thurman, during 1985–1986. It was subsequently taken up by General John R. Galvin, commander in chief, U.S. Southern Command; General Fred F. Woerner, Jr.; and others during 1986–1995. The resultant model, originally called SSI 1 and SSI 2, has also been called the SWORD model and the Manwaring Paradigm. The model predicts at an impressive 88.37 percent and is statistically significant at the 0.001 level. The SWORD Papers, although long out of print, are archived in their entirety by a private research organization, the National Security Archives, in Washington, DC.

13. Ibid.

14. Robert K. Yin, *Case Study Research: Design and Methods*, 2nd ed. (Thousand Oaks, CA: SAGE Publications), pp. 138–139.

15. Clausewitz, *On War*, 1976.

16. Kennan, "Morality and Foreign Policy," Winter 1985–1986.

17. Antonio de Spinola, *Ao Servicio de Portugal* (Lisbon: Atica/Livraria Bertrand, 1976), pp. 9–24; and Antonio de Spinola, *Portugal e o futuro* (Lisbon: Arcadia, 1974), pp. 130–270. Additionally, *Author Interviews* were conducted in Lisbon, Portugal, October 17–19, 1985; October 1–4, 1987; February 19–21, 1990; and July 9–16, 2006. Hereafter cited as *Author Interviews*. These and subsequent assertions are based on the author's Field Notes, Portugal, 1986–1991. These notes include interviews with 30 senior military and civilian officials and are cited as *Author Interviews*.

18. Tony Judt, *Postwar: A History of Europe since 1945* (New York: Penguin Press, 2005), pp. 510–512. Also see A.H. de Oliveira Marques, *A History of Portugal* (New York: Columbia University Press, 1976), p. 162; Kenneth Maxwell, "The Emergence of Portuguese Democracy," in John H. Herz, ed., *From Dictatorship to Democracy* (Westport, CN: Greenwood Press, 1982), pp. 231–250; and *Author Interviews*.

19. Ibid. Also see Rona M. Fields, *The Portuguese Revolution and the Armed Forces Movement* (New York: Praeger, 1976), p. 200; Thomas C. Bruneau, "Portugal: Problems and Prospects in the Creation of a New Regime,"*Naval War College Review*, Summer 1976, pp. 65–83; and *Author Interviews*.

20. Ibid.; and *Author Interviews*.

21. Ibid.; and Spinola, *Ao Servicio de Portugal*, 1976; Spinola, *Portugal e o futuro*, 1974; and *Author Interviews*.

22. Ibid.

23. Ibid.

24. Michael Howard, "The Forgotten Dimensions of Strategy," *The Causes of War* (London: Temple-Smith, 1981), pp. 101–115.

25. Ibid.; Spinola, *Portugal e o futuro*, 1974; and *Author Interviews*.

26. Spinola, *Ao Servicio de Portugal*, 1976.

27. Ibid.

28. Ibid.

29. Ibid.

30. Niccolo Machiavelli, *The Art of War* (New York: Da Capo Press, 1965), pp. 7–8, 84–85, 122–123.

CHAPTER 2

1. Daniel C. Esty, Ted Robert Gurr, Barbara Harff, and Pamela Surko, "The State Failure Project: Early Warning Research for U.S. Policy Planning," in John Davies and Ted Robert Gurr, eds., *Preventive Measures: Building a Risk Assessment and Crisis Early Warning Systems* (New York: Rowman and Littlefield, 1998), pp. 27–38.

2. Carl von Clausewitz, *On War*, ed. and trans. Michael Howard and Peter Paret (Princeton, NJ: Princeton University Press, 1976), p. 596.

3. See www.unglobalcompact.org; *Millennium Report: Responsibility to Protect* (New York: International Commission on Intervention and State Sovereignty, August 15, 2001); and http://www.oas.org/en/sms/docs/declaration%20security%20americas%20rev%201%20-%2028%20oct%202003%20ce00339.pdf.

4. Boutros Boutros-Ghali, *An Agenda for Peace* (New York: United Nations, 1992); and "Global Leadership after the Cold War," *Foreign Affairs*, March/April 1996, pp. 86–98.

5. Max G. Manwaring and John T. Fishel, "Insurgency and Counter-Insurgency: Toward a New Analytical Model," *Small Wars and Insurgencies* (Winter 1992), pp. 272–310.

6. Ibid. Also see John T. Fishel and Max G. Manwaring, *Uncomfortable Wars Revisited* (Norman, OK: University of Oklahoma Press, 2006), pp. 37–38, 66–70, 132–133, 204–205.

7. Boutros Boutros-Ghali, *An Agenda for Peace*, 1992; and "Global Leadership after the Cold War," 1996.

8. Vittorfranco Pisano, *The Dynamics of Subversion and Violence in Contemporary Italy* (Stanford, DA: Hoover Institution Press, 1987), pp. 5–40.

9. Donatella Della Porta, "Left-Wing Terrorism in Italy," in Martha Crenshaw, ed., *Terrorism in Context* (University Park, PA: Penn State University Press, 1995), pp. 105–139; Richard Drake, *The Aldo Moro Murder Case* (Cambridge, MA: Harvard University Press, 1995), pp. 50–51; Declaration of Red Brigades sent to *L'Expresso* and published as *"Le due anieme delle Br,"* March 1, 1989; Enrico Fenzi, *Armi e Bagagli: Un diario delle Brigae Rossa* (Genova: Cosa and Nolan, 1987), p. 76; Sue Ellen Moran, *A Rand Note: Court Deposition of Three Red Brigadists* (Sana Monica, CA: Rand, February 1986), pp. 47, 59–60; and *Author Interviews*. These and subsequent assertions are based on the author's Field Notes, Italy, 1986–1991. These notes include interviews with 20 junior and senior paramilitary and civilian officials and are cited as *Author Interviews*.

10. Ibid.; and Pisano, *The Dynamics of Subversion and Violence in Contemporary Italy*, 1987.

11. Ibid.

12. Ibid.

13. *Author Interviews*. Also see Niccolo Machiavelli, *The Art of War* (New York: DeCapo Press, 1965), pp. liv–livi, 7–8, 34–36, 46, 77–78, 171, 179, 202–204.

14. *Author Interviews*.

15. Ibid.; and Pisano, *The Dynamics of Subversion and Violence in Contemporary Italy*, 1987.

16. Interview with militant quoted in Della Porta, "Left-Wing Terrorism in Italy," 1995.

17. *Author Interviews*.

18. Ibid.; and Della Porta, "Left-Wing Terrorism in Italy," 1995.

19. Ibid.; also see Fishel and Manwaring, *Uncomfortable Wars Revisited*, 2006.

20. Ibid.

21. Pisano, *The Dynamics of Subversion and Violence in Contemporary Italy*, 1987; Della Porta, "Left-Wing Terrorism in Italy," 1995; and *Author Interviews*.

22. General (UK) Sir Rupert Smith, *The Utility of Force: The Art of War in the Modern World* (New York: Alfred A. Knopf, 2007), pp. 3, 145.

23. Janos Besyno, *Western Sahara* (Budapest, Hungary, 2009). Self-authored report presented to the chief of staff of the Hungarian army on his return from duty with the UN peacekeeping effort in Western Sahara (MINUSO).

24. Ibid.

25. Ibid.

26. Rick Gladstone, "Morocco Asks That U.N. Close Western Sahara Military Office," *New York Times*, March 22, 2016, p. A–8.

27. George F. Kennan, "Morality and Foreign Policy," *Foreign Affairs*, Winter 1985–1986, pp. 205–218.

28. Clausewitz, *On War*, 1976, p. 596.

29. Sun Tzu, *The Art of War*, trans. Samuel B. Griffith (Oxford: Oxford University Press, 1963), p. 61.

CHAPTER 3

1. See for example: Max G. Manwaring and John T. Fishel, "Insurgency and Counter-Insurgency: Toward a New Analytical Model," *Small Wars and Insurgencies* (Winter 1992), pp. 272–310. Also see John P. Sullivan and Robert J. Bunker, "Drug Cartels, Street Gangs, and Warlords," *Non-State Threats and Future Wars* (London: Frank Cass, 2003), pp. 40–53.

2. Lewis Carroll, *Alice's Adventures in Wonderland & through the Looking Glass* (New York: Bantam Books, 1981), p. 46.

3. *Author Interviews* with General John R. Galvin (Ret., U.S. Army), August 6, 1997, Boson, MA; General Anthony Zinni (U.S. Marine Corps, commander in chief, the U.S. Central Command), June 2, 1999, and October 6, 2000, Washington, DC; General Charles E. Wilhelm (Ret., U.S. Marine Corps), February 9, 2001, and June 2, 2001, Washington, DC; and Lieutenant General William G. Carter III (Ret., U.S. Army), November 30, 1998, and March 2, 1999, Washington, DC.

4. Ibid.

5. Ibid.

6. Bruce B. G. Clark, "End-State Planning: The Somalia Case," in Max G. Manwaring and William J. Olson, eds., *Managing Contemporary Conflict: Pillars of Success* (Boulder, CO: Westview Press, 1996), pp. 49–69. Also see Carroll, *Alice's Adventures in Wonderland & through the Looking Glass*, 1981, p. 46.

7. *Author Interviews.*

8. Steven D. Krasner and Carlos Pascual, "Addressing State Failure," *Foreign Affairs*, July–August 2005, pp. 153–155.

9. Max G. Manwaring, "Executive Summary. U.S. Forces, Somalia," *After Action Report* (Carlisle Barracks, PA: U.S. Army Peacekeeping Institute, 1994).

10. Ibid. Also see John T. Fishel, "The Challenge of Peace Enforcement in Somalia," in John T. Fishel and Max G. Manwaring, eds., *Uncomfortable Wars Revisited* (Norman, OK: University of Oklahoma Press, 2006), pp. 204–209, 228–230.

11. Ibid.

12. *Terms of Reference (TOR) for U.S. Forces in Somalia*, April 1993.

13. Fishel, "The Challenge of Peace Enforcement in Somalia," (2006), pp. 204–209; 228–230.

14. Ibid., pp. 206–209, 228–230. Also see Manwaring, "Executive Summary. U.S. Forces, Somalia," 1994.

15. Ibid.

16. Ibid.

17. General Rupert Smith, *The Utility of Force* (New York: Alfred A. Knopf, 2007), pp. 336–348. Also see Max G. Manwaring, *Bosnia-Herzegovina after Action Review (BHAAR 1) Conference Report* (Carlisle Barracks, PA: U.S. Army Peacekeeping Institute, May 19–23, 1996); and Max G. Manwaring, *Bosnia-Herzegovina after Action Review (BHAAR II) Conference Report* (Carlisle Barracks, PA: U.S. Army Peacekeeping Institute, April 13–17, 1997).

18. Ibid.

19. Ibid.

20. Ibid.

21. Ibid.

22. Ibid.

23. Ibid.

24. *Author Interviews* with General Carter, November 30, 1998, and March 2, 1999, Washington, DC.

25. Carl von Clausewitz, *On War*, ed. and trans. Michael Howard and Peter Paret (Princeton, NJ: Princeton University Press, 1976), p. 596.

CHAPTER 4

1. Jean-Jacques Rousseau, *The Social Contract and Other Later Political Writings*, trans. Victor Gourevitch (Cambridge, England: Cambridge University Press, 1997), pp. 39–152.

2. Boutros Boutros-Ghali, "Global Leadership after the Cold War," *Foreign Affairs*, March/April 1996, pp. 86–98.

3. Max G. Manwaring and John T. Fishel, "Insurgency and Counter-Insurgency: Toward a New Analytical Model," *Small Wars and Insurgencies* (Winter 1992), pp. 272–310. Also see Edwin G. Corr and Max G. Manwaring, "Confronting the New World Disorder," in Max G. Manwaring and William. J. Olson, eds., *Managing Contemporary Conflict: Pillars of Success* (Boulder, CO: Westview Press, 1996), pp. 86–98; and also see Note 11, Chapter 1.

4. Ibid.

5. Ibid.

6. Carl von Clausewitz, *On War*, ed. and trans. Michael Howard and Peter Paret (Princeton, NJ: Princeton University Press, 1976), pp. 75–89.

7. Ibid., pp. 75–89, 596. Also see Jacques Maritain, *Man and the State* (Chicago, IL: University of Chicago Press, 1963), p. 19.

8. Ibid.

9. Sun Tzu, *The Art of War*, trans. Samuel B. Griffith (Oxford: Oxford University Press, 1963), p. 79; and Joseph S. Nye, Jr., "Restoring American Leadership through Smart Power," *Global Strategic Assessment* (Washington, DC: National Defense University, Institute for National Strategic Studies, 2009), pp. 474–476.

10. Qiao Liang and Wang Xiangsui, *Unrestricted Warfare* (Beijing: PLA Literature and Arts Publishing House, 1999), pp. 305–306.

11. Amitai Etzioni, "Responsibility as Sovereignty," *Orbis* (Winter 2006), pp. 1–15. Also see Amitai Etzioni, "Changing the Rules," *Foreign Affairs*, November/December 2011, p. 173.

12. George F. Kennan, "The Sources of Soviet Conduct," *Foreign Affairs*, July 1947, pp. 566–582.

13. Joseph N. McBride, "America Coping with Chaos at the Strategic Level," in Max G. Manwaring and James Joes, eds., *Beyond Declaring Victory and Coming Home* (Westport, CN: Praeger, 2000), pp. 214–215.

14. Guillermo E. Gini, "Piqueteros: De la protesta social a la accion politica," *Estrategia* (CIFE, September 2004), pp. 60–66.

15. *Author Interviews* and observations. Also see Isabella Alcaniz and Melissa Scheier, "New Social Movements with Old Party Politics: The MTL *Piqueteros* and the Communist Party of Argentina," *Latin American Perspectives* 34, no. 2 (2007), pp. 157–171; Ana Dinerstein, "Power or Counter-Power? The Dilemma of the *Piquetero* Movement in Argentina Post-Crisis," *Capital and Class* 81 (Autumn 2003), pp. 1–7.

16. V. I. Lenin, "Tasks of Russian Social-Democrats," *The Lenin Anthology*, 1975, pp. 3–11; and "What Is to Be Done?" *The Lenin Anthology*, 1975, pp. 12–114.

17. *Author Interviews*. Also see Ana Dinerstein, "Power or Counter-Power? The Dilemma of the *Piquetero* Movement in Argentina Post-Crisis," *Capital and Class* 81 (Autumn 2003), pp. 1–7.

18. Michael Howard, *The Lessons of History* (New Haven, CT: Yale University Press, 1991), p. 3.

19. *Author Interviews*. Also note John P. Sullivan, "Terrorism, Crime, and Private Armies," *Low Intensity Conflict & Law Enforcement* (Winter 2002), pp. 239–253.

20. Ibid.

21. Ibid.

22. Ambassador David C. Jordan, *Drug Politics: Dirty Money and Democracies* (Norman, OK: University of Oklahoma Press, 1999), pp. 158–170, 193–194.

CHAPTER 5

1. General Vo Nguyen Giap, *People's War, People's Army* (New York: Praeger, 1962), pp. 34–36.

2. Harry G. Summers, Jr., *On Strategy: The Vietnam War in Context* (Carlisle Barracks, PA: Strategic Studies Institute, 1989), p. 1.

3. Max G. Manwaring and Edwin G. Corr, "Confronting the New World Disorder: A Legitimate Governance Theory of Engagement," in Max G. Manwaring and Wm. J. Olson, eds., *Managing Contemporary Conflict: Pillars of Success* (Boulder, CO: Westview Press, 1996), pp. 31–47. Also see Note 11, Chapter 1.

4. Stephen D. Krasner and Carlos Pascual, "Addressing State Failure," *Foreign Affairs*, July–August 2005, pp. 153–155.

5. Ibid.

6. Ibid.

7. Ibid.; also see Max G. Manwaring, *Ambassador Stephen Krasner's Orienting Principle for Foreign Policy (and Military Management)—Responsible Sovereignty* (Carlisle Barracks, PA: Strategic Studies Institute, 2012), pp. 1–44.

8. *Author Interviews* with General Anthony Zinni (U.S. Marine Corps, commander in chief, the U.S. Central Command), June 2, 1999, Washington, DC; General John R. Galvin (Ret., U.S. Army), August 6, 1997, Boston, MA (the complete interview is included in the Spring 1998 special issue of *Small Wars and Insurgencies*);

and Lieutenant General William G. Carter, III (Ret., U.S. Army), November 30, 1998, and March 2, 1999, Washington, DC. Also see Boutros Boutros-Ghali, "Global Leadership after the Cold War," *Foreign Affairs*, March/April 1994, pp. 86–98.

9. Max G. Manwaring and John T. Fishel, "Insurgency and Counter-Insurgency: Toward a New Analytical Model," *Small Wars and Insurgencies* (Winter 1992), pp. 272–310.

10. Bernard Fall, "Indochina, 1946–1954," and "South Vietnam, 1956 to November 1963," in D. M. Condi, et al., eds., *Challenge and Response in Internal Conflict: The Experience in Asia*, Volume I (Washington, DC: The American University Center for Research in Social Systems, 1968), pp. 237–266, 333–369; and *Author Interviews*.

11. Summers, *On Strategy*, 1989, p. 1.

12. Carl von Clausewitz, *On War*, ed. and trans. Michael Howard and Peter Paret (Princeton, NJ: Princeton University Press, 1976; Orig. pub. 1832), pp. 88–89.

13. Qiao Liang and Wang Xiangsui, *Unrestricted Warfare* (Beijing: PLA Literature and Arts Publishing House, 1999), pp. 25, 133.

14. Ibid.

15. Michael Howard, "The Forgotten Dimensions of Strategy," in M. Howard, eds., *The Causes of War* (London: Temple-Smith, 1981), p. 110.

16. Summers, *On Strategy*, 1989; also see General Giap, *People's War, People's Army*, 1962, pp. 34–36.

17. Ibid.; also see Former Secretary of Defense Robert McNamara in David K. Shipler, "Robert McNamara Meets the Enemy," *New York Times Magazine*, August 10, 1997, p. 50.

18. Ibid.; and *Author Interviews*.

19. Clausewitz, *On War*, 1976, p. 596.

20. Frank Hoffman, *Conflict in the 21st Century: The Rise of Hybrid Wars* (Arlington, VA: Potomac Institute for Policy Studies, December 2007), pp. 5–10; also see Matthew Connelly, "Rethinking the Cold War and Decolonization: The Grand Strategy of the Algerian War for Independence," *International Journal of Middle Eastern Studies* 33 (2001), pp. 221–245; Roger Trinquier, *Modern Warfare: A French View of Counterinsurgency* (Barcelona, Spain; n.p., 1965), pp. 31–34; Manuel Ortega, "Antecedentes de la guerra asimetrica: la guerra revolucionaria en Arglia," annex 6 in Jorge Verstrynge Rojas, eds., *La guerra periferica* (Madrid: El Viejo Topo, 2005), p. 165; and *Author Interviews*.

21. Ibid.; also see Edgar S. Furniss, Jr., *DeGaulle and the French Army: A Crisis in Civil-Military Relations* (New York: Twentieth Century Fund, 1964), p. 25; and Anthony James Joes, "French Algeria: the Victory and the Crucifixion of an Army," in James Joes, ed., *From the Barrel of a Gun: Armies and Revolutions* (Washington, DC: Pergamon-Brassey's, 1986), pp. 139–158.

22. Ibid.

23. Jean Larteguy, *The Centurions* (New York: E.P. Dutton, 1961), pp. 181–182.

CHAPTER 6

1. Thomas Hobbes, "Of Commonwealth," Chapter XVII in Saxe Commins and Robert Linscott, eds., *Man and the State: The Political Philosophers* (New York: Modern Pocket Library, 1953), pp. 3–54; also see Jean-Jacques Rousseau, *The Social*

Contract and Other Later Political Writings, trans. Victor Gourevitch (Cambridge: Cambridge University Press, 1997), pp. 39–152.

2. Ibid.

3. Max G. Manwaring and John T. Fishel, "Insurgency and Counter Insurgency: Toward a New Analytical Approach," *Small Wars & Insurgencies* (Winter 1992), pp. 272–310; also see Note 11, Chapter 1.

4. Ibid.

5. Ibid.

6. *Author Interviews* with General Sir Robert Thompson, January 16, 1986, Washington, DC.

7. Manwaring and Fishel, "Insurgency and Counter Insurgency," 1992, pp. 272–310.

8. George F. Kennan, "Morality and Foreign Policy," *Foreign Affairs*, Winter 1985–1986, pp. 205–218.

9. *Author Interviews* with Thompson, 1986.

10. Ibid.

11. Ibid.

12. Jacques Maritain, *Man and the State* (Chicago, IL: University of Chicago Press, 1963), p. 19.

13. Ernesto "Che" Guevara, *Guerrilla Warfare* (New York: Monthly Review Press, 1961), pp. 15–20; also see V. I. Lenin, "Symptoms of a Revolutionary Situation," in Robert C. Tucker, ed., *The Lenin Anthology* (New York: W.W. Norton, 1975), pp. 275–277.

14. Ibid.

15. Joaquin Villalobos, "El estado actual de la guerra y sus perexpectivas," *ECA: Estudios Centroamericanos* 499 (March 1986), pp. 169–204; and *Author Interviews* with Miguel Castallanos (former FMLN commander), September 1987, San Salvador; interview with President Duarte, November 1987, San Salvador; and interview with Ambassador Edwin G. Corr, June 2011, Washington, DC, and others for nonattribution. Note the assertions made here and later are the result of interviews with more than 40 senior Salvadoran civilian and military officials conducted over the period between October 1986 and December 1987 in El Salvador, Panama, and the United States (hereafter cited as *Nonattribution Interviews*).

16. Ibid.

17. Ibid.

18. On October 11, 1980, the Unified Revolutionary Directorate (DRU) announced the founding of the Farabundo Marti National Liberation Front (FMLN). It was made up of the Popular Liberation Forces—Farabundo Marti, the People's Army, and the Armed Forces for National Liberation. On November 11, the Armed Forces of National Resistance were also incorporated into the FMLN. *Nonattribution Interviews*.

19. Ibid.

20. Ibid.

21. Marta Harnecker, "From Insurrection to War: An Interview with Joaquin Villalobos," in M. Dixon and S. Jonas, eds., *Revolution and Intervention* (San Francisco: Synthesis Publications, 1983), pp. 40–46, 70–71.

22. *Author Interviews* with Dr. Guillermo M. Ungo (representing the Democratic Revolutionary Front, [FDR]), December 11, 1987, Panama City, Panama.

23. *Nonattribution Interviews.*

24. *Author Interviews* with Dr. Alvaro Magana (former provisional president of El Salvador), December 1986, June and November 1987, and February, July, and October 1989, San Salvador.

25. *Author Interviews* with General John R. Galvin (Commander in Chief, U.S. Southern Command, 1985–1987), August 1987, Mons, Belgium.

26. *Author Interviews* with Ambassador Edwin G. Corr (U.S. Ambassador to El Salvador), June and September 1987, San Salvador; also see Edwin G. Corr, "The Salvadoran Report Card," in Max G. Manwaring and Court Prisk, eds., *El Salvador at War: An Oral History* (Washington, DC: National Defense University Press, 1988), pp. 452–453.

CHAPTER 7

1. Max G. Manwaring and John T. Fishel, "Insurgency and Counter-Insurgency: Toward a New Analytical Model," *Small Wars and Insurgencies* (Winter 1992), pp. 272–310; also see Note 11, Chapter 1.

2. Abraham Guillen, *Philosophy of the Urban Guerrilla: The Revolutionary Writings of Abraham Guillen* (New York: William Morrow, 1973), pp. 278–279.

3. Manwaring and Fishel, "Insurgency and Counter-Insurgency," 1992.

4. Carlos Gueron, "Introduction," in Joseph S. Tulchin, ed., *Venezuela in the Wake of Radical Reform* (Boulder, CO: Lynne Rienner Publishers, 1993), pp. 1–3.

5. Hubert Herring, *A History of Latin America* (New York: Alfred A. Knopf, 1972), pp. 513–514.

6. *Author Interviews.*

7. *Author Interviews*; also see *The Economist*, "Special Report: Hugo Chavez's Venezuela," May 14, 2005, pp. 23–24; *The Economist*, "The Chavez Machine Rolls On," December 2, 2006, pp. 41–42; and *The Economist*, "Chavez Victorious," December 9, 2006; and Steve Ellner, "Revolutionary and Non-Revolutionary Paths of Radical Populism: Directions of Chavez Movement in Venezuela," *Science and Society* (April 2005), pp. 160–190.

8. Jean-Jacques Rousseau, *The Social Contract and Other Later Political Writings*, trans. Victor Gourevitch (Cambridge: Cambridge University Press, 1997), pp. 39–161; and Jacques Maritain, *Man and the State* (Chicago, IL: University of Chicago Press, 1951), pp. 13–27, 192.

9. Ibid.

10. Michael Shifter, "In Search of Hugo Chavez," *Foreign Affairs*, May/June 2006, p. 46.

11. *Author Interviews.*

12. General Gustavo Reyes Rangel Biceno's speech when he accepted the post of *Ministro del Poder Popular para la Defensa* (the paramilitary forces of Venezuela), July 18, 2007; and International Crisis Group, "Violence and Politics in Venezuela—Militias," Latin America Report No. 38, August 17, 2011, pp. 26–27.

13. Joseph M. Humire's (Executive Director, Center for a Secure Society [SFS]) written testimony before the U.S. House of Representatives Committee on Foreign

Affairs Subcommittee on the Western Hemisphere hearing on "Issues and Opportunities in the Western Hemisphere," February 28, 2017.

14. President Chavez used this language in a charge to the National Armed
Forces (FAN) to develop a doctrine for fourth-generation war, asymmetric war of
all the people, and super insurgency interchangeably. See *El Universal*, April 8,
2005.

15. V. I. Lenin said that a "new society" will only be created by gradual and
systematic application of agitation and propaganda. See V. I. Lenin, "The Tasks
of the Russian Social Democrats," in Robert C. Tucker, ed., *The Lenin Anthology*
(New York: W.W. Norton & Company, 1975), pp. 4–7; "Speech in Closing the
Congress," *The Lenin Anthology*, 1975, p. 533; "Socialism and War," *The Lenin
Anthology*, 1975, p. 188; and "The State and Revolution," *The Lenin Anthology*,
1975, p. 324.

16. For one example, see Megan Specia, "Migrant Flow into Ecuador Acceler-
ates," *New York Times*, August 12, 2018, p. 7.

17. *Latinobarometro, Informe* (Santiago, Chile: Latinobarometro Corporation,
2017), pp. 50–59; also see Meridith Kohut, "Keeping a Grip on Venezuela, Using
Food," *New York Times*, May 20, 2018, p. 10; Mercy Benzaquen, "How Food in Venezuela Went from Subsidized to Scarce," *New York Times*, July 24, 2017, p. A10; Kirk
Semple, "In a Venezuela Ravaged by Inflation, a Race for Survival," *New York
Times*, December 3, 2017, p. 9; Enrique Krause, "Stop Totalitarianism in Venezuela," *New York Times*, June 29, 2017, Op. Ed.; Mathew Hoag, "Chef Draws Ire
on Menu for President of Venezuela," *New York Times*, September 19, 2018, p. A7;
and Ernesto Londono and Nicholas Casey, "U.S. Met Rebels from Venezuela about
Coup Plot," *New York Times*, September 9, 2018, pp. 1, 11.

18. Albert Camus, *The Rebel* (New York: Vintage Books, 1956), pp. 302–306.

19. F. A. Godfrey, "The Latin American Experience: The Tupamaros Campaigns in Uruguay, 1963–1973," in Ian F. W. Beckett and John Pimlott, eds., *Armed
Forces and Modern Counter-Insurgency* (New York: St. Martin's Press, 2001), pp. 112–
135. Also note that from 1955 through 2006, the author was in a position from
which to observe the situation in Uruguay and interview civilian and military officials in that country. Thus, this and subsequent assertions made in this chapter are
consensus statements based on observation and interviews hereafter cited as
Author Interviews.

20. Ibid.; also see Liza Gross, "Uruguay—Movimiento de Liberacion Nacional
Tupamaros," in *Handbook of Leftist Guerrilla Groups in Latin America and the Caribbean* (Boulder, CO: Westview Press, 1995), pp. 145–149.

21. *Author Interviews*.

22. Ibid.; also see Diego Abante, "Uruguay—Democracy: Idea, Practice, and
Tradition of Co-participation," in Jan Kippers Black, ed., *Latin America: Its Problems
and Promise* (Boulder, CO: Westview Press, 1984), pp. 453–458.

23. According to many Latin Americans, Rodo's writings were widely read
and discussed from Mexico and the Antilles to Argentina and Chile. A. Curtis Wilgus stated that such writings as *Ariel* and the *Motives of Proteus* came to be virtually
holy scripture to many of the young men and women of the United States in the
mid-1900s and again in the early 2000s. William Rex Crawford observed that Ariel
became "the "pillow book" for Uruguayan and other South American youth after

Rodo's death in 1917. During his residence in Uruguay, Wilgus observed the same phenomenon as Crawford. See A. Curtis Wilgus, *Modern Hispanic-America* (Washington, D.C.: George Washington University Press, 1933), pp. 196–197; and William Rex Crawford, *A Century of Latin American Thought* (Cambridge, MA: Harvard University Press, 1961), p. 79.

24. *Author Interviews.* Also see Abante, "Uruguay—Democracy," 1984; Godfrey, "The Latin American Experience," 2001; Gross, "Uruguay—Movimiento de Liberacion Nacional Tupamaros," 1995.

25. Ibid.

26. Abraham Guillen, "Philosophy of the Urban Guerrilla," in *The Revolutionary Writings of Abraham Guillen*, trans. Donald C. Hodges (New York: William Morrow, 1973), pp. 267–273.

27. *Author Interviews.*

28. *Author Interviews.*

29. *Author Interviews.*

CHAPTER 8

1. Bruce Riedel, *What We Won* (Washington, DC: Brookings Institution, 2014), p. 156. He was a member of the National Security Council and a CIA veteran who was present at the conflict.

2. Jacques Maritain, *Man and the State* (Chicago, IL: University of Chicago Press, 1951), pp. 18–19.

3. Joseph S. Nye, Jr., "Restoring American Leadership through Smart Power," *Global Strategic Assessment* (Washington, DC: National Defense University, Institute for National Strategic Studies, 2009), pp. 474–476.

4. Qiao Liang and Wang Xiangsui, *Unrestricted Warfare* (Beijing: PLA Literature and Arts Publishing House, 1999), pp. 38, 154.

5. *Author Interviews* with Lt. General William G. Carter, III, November 1998 and March 1999, Washington, DC. He was the commander of U.S. and NATO forces in Bosnia in the mid-1990s.

6. Boutros Boutros-Ghali, "Global Leadership after the Cold War, *Foreign Affairs*, March/April 1996, pp. 86–98, 90–93.

7. As examples of this discussion, see Francis F. Ding, et al., *Sovereignty as Responsibility* (Washington, DC: The Brookings Institution, 1996), p. 33; Lee Feinstein and Ann-Marie Slaughter, "A Duty to Prevent," *Foreign Affairs*, January/February 2004, pp. 136–150; Amitai Etzioni, "Responsibility and Sovereignty," *Orbis*, Winter 2006, pp. 1–15; and Mohammed Ayoob, "Defining Security: A Subaltern Realist Perspective," in Keith Krause and Michael C. Williams, eds., *Critical Security Studies* (Minneapolis, MN: University of Minnesota Press, 1997), pp. 121–146.

8. Carl von Clausewitz, *On War* (Princeton, NJ: Princeton University Press, 1976), pp. 80–89.

9. George F. Kennan, "The Sources of Soviet Conduct," *Foreign Affairs*, July 1947, pp. 556–582.

10. Colonel T. X. Hammes (Ret., U.S. Marine Corps), *The Sling and the Stone* (Grand Rapids, MI: Zenith Press, 2006), pp. 209–210, 246–257.

11. Ibid.; also see General Rupert Smith (Ret., UK), *The Utility of Force: The Art of War in the Modern World* (New York: Alfred A. Knopf, 2007), pp. 374–385.

12. David C. Miller, Jr., "Structuring Foreign Policy in a Post–Cold War World," in Max G. Manwaring and William J. Olson, eds., *Managing Contemporary Conflict; Pillars of Success* (Boulder, CO: Westview Press, 1996), pp. 13–28.

13. Ibid.

14. Max G. Manwaring, *Ambassador Stephen Krasner's Orienting Principle for Foreign Policy (and Military Management)—Responsible Sovereignty* (Carlisle Barracks, PA: Strategic Studies Institute, 2012), pp. 1–44.; David Easton, *The Political System: An Inquiry into the State of Political Science* (New York: Knopf, 1963), pp. 99, 218–219; Thomas Homer-Dixon, "On the Threshold: Environmental Changes as Causes of Acute Conflict," *International Security* 16, no. 2 (Fall 1991), pp. 114–115; and Amitai Etzioni, "Changing the Rules," *Foreign Affairs*, November/December 2011, p. 173.

15. Ibid.

16. See Note 11, Chapter 1.

17. Albert Camus, *The Rebel* (New York: Vintage Books, 1956), pp. 275–277.

18. V. I. Lenin, "The Lenin Anthology," in Robert C. Tucker, ed., *The State and Revolution* (New York: W.W. Norton, 1975), p. 324.

19. V. I. Lenin, "The Lenin Anthology," in Robert C. Tucker, ed., *The Fall of the Old and the Fight for the New* (New York: W.W. Norton, 1975), p. 425.

20. Tony Judt, *Postwar: A History of Europe since 1945* (New York: Penguin Press, 2005), pp. 551, 590–591, 593.

21. Ibid.; Riedel, *What We Won*, 2014, pp. xiv, 6, 13, 19, 24–26, 46, 51.

22. Ibid.

23. Ibid.

24. Ibid.; also see Gustavo de Aristegui, *La Yihad en Espana: La obsesion por reconquistar Al-Andalus*, 5th ed. (Madrid: La Esfera de los Libros, 2006).

25. Ibid.; and *Author Interviews* with members of the Spanish parliament, July 5–8, 2006, Madrid, Spain.

26. Ibid.

27. Ibid.

28. Sun Tzu, *The Art of War*, trans. Samuel B. Griffith (Oxford: Oxford University Press, 1963), p. 143.

Index

About the Author

MAX G. MANWARING, PhD, is a retired professor of military strategy at the Strategic Studies Institute (SSI) of the U.S. Army War College (USAWC), where he has held the General Douglas MacArthur Chair of Research, and is a retired U.S. Army colonel. Over the past 30-plus years, he has served in various military and civilian positions. They include the U.S. Southern Command, the Defense Intelligence Agency, Dickinson College, and the University of Memphis. Dr. Manwaring is the author and coauthor of several articles, chapters, and books dealing with intranational and international security affairs, political-military affairs, insurgency, counterinsurgency, and gangs. His most recent book is *The Complexity of Modern Irregular War* (University of Oklahoma Press, 2012). His most recent publication is a chapter entitled "Revolutionary Armed Forces of Colombia (FARC): A Transnational Criminal-Insurgent-Terror Phenomenon," in Kimberley L. Thachuk and Rollie Lal, eds., *Terrorist Criminal Enterprises: Financing Terrorism through Organized Crime* (Praeger, 2018). Dr. Manwaring remains active in the national security community.